Still Stories

Hans Offringa

Still Stories

From Kentucky to Kilbeggan

Conceptual Continuity

© 2016 Hans Offringa
© 2016 Conceptual Continuity

Photography:
The Whisky Couple, excepting
p. 50 – Kick Visser
pp. 106, 133 – Marcel Langedijk

Graphic design advice: Laurien Stam
Editing and layout: Becky Lovett Offringa

ISBN 978-90-78668-33-6

www.hansoffringa.com
www.thewhiskycouple.com
www.conceptualcontinuity.nl

Table of Contents

Foreword

The first time I met Hans Offringa must have been in 2004. I stayed with my wife in the Scottish Craigellachie Hotel where Hans was signing copies of *The Road to Craigellachie* in the famous Quaich Bar. He was sitting in a corner of the bar, behind a small table covered with a stack of books and a glass of Lagavulin Double Matured in front of him, totally beleaguered by a friendly but very pushy Japanese lady, for whom he had just signed a copy of his book. I instantly decided to save him and offered him a dram.

Thankfully he escaped the intentions of the eager Japanese lady, who seemed to have big plans with him and left the bar rather disappointedly. Hans and I soon engaged in a lively conversation and were in for a historic evening with his friend and mentor Michael Jackson in the hotel's library. The 'late and great' Michael, who has had a great influence on Hans' work and career.

Our first encounter marked the beginning of a long friendship and cooperation. It led to our joint project *The Legend of Laphroaig* and a few publications outside the whisky world, for which I acted as the photographer-in-residence. Our cooperation wasn't smooth at all times. We regularly clashed, having different opinions and ideas. Where Hans sometimes ventured slightly from the world of facts to spice up a dry story, I would lose myself during research in correct, but utterly boring details that might encumber the readability of the forthcoming book.

Luckily there was always his muse Becky, the cement in our artistic relationship. With her trademark subtlety she always managed to bring us and our ideas together. It created a field of tension, in which creativity could fully bloom and where beautiful things come into being. We learned how to approach and also learned from one another.

The Legend of Laphroaig is a book we both feel proud of. Charles Maclean mentioned it a 'benchmark' for historical books about distilleries. What more to wish for? After the launch of the publication, we continued to work together. I would read manuscripts of books to come and commented on them, very honest and not always tactful, though with respect. But Hans never stays angry and can take criticism well. He uses it to his benefit. The end result for him is more important than his Frisian pride.

Sure, he has a thorough understanding and knowledge about whisky, and about bourbon. But above all Hans is a master of language, in Dutch and in English, and he has a lot to tell. His work brings him to the most beautiful places on earth and together with Becky he meets the most colourful and eclectic people.

In *Still Stories* he returned to the path he took with *The Road to Craigellachie.* I cannot escape mentioning that book, since for many whisky lovers it has been their first acquaintance with Scotland and whisky. That book was the first building block for Hans' reputation as a whisky writer worldwide. I enjoy his writing in this genre, he is a born storyteller. Hans writes in a clear and very accessible style, with which he distinguishes himself from many among his colleagues.

Still Stories has the same agreeable recognition as *The Road*, but is enriched with more facts and well-documented nice-to-knows and need-to-knows. It also shows his growth as an author. This book is a welcome distraction from the plethora of new, often too technical books on the topic, repeating themselves over and over. It is an entertaining and utterly digestible collection of stories about people, about events, about whisky and bourbon, augmented with historical backgrounds.

The author takes the reader, often with tongue-in-cheek humour, from the USA to Scotland, ending his tour in Ireland. The accent might for an extent have been shifted from whisky to bourbon. A direction Hans took a few years ago with his award-winning book *Bourbon & Blues*. Well, it's logical for a couple that permanently commutes between The Netherlands and that other country, from where Becky originates, and where Hans feels at home too: the USA, cradle of bourbon.

I really enjoyed reading *Still Stories* and cordially recommend it. Oh, don't believe everything Hans has written about me in the chapter 'The Making of ...' Everything for a good story, Frodo!

Marcel van Gils.

Note from the author:
When Marcel sent me the above foreword early 2014, for the Dutch edition, neither of us knew that we would team up again at the end of that year for *The Legend of Laphroaig*'s sequel *1815-2015 – 200 Years of Laphroaig*.

Introduction

For years I have been relishing the many emails received from the whisky lovers who asked if I wanted to write a sequel to *The Road to Craigellachie*. Of course I wanted that, but for quite some time I wasn't entirely sure how to approach the project. Did it have to be The Road to Kentucky, or a story about my whisky adventures in the USA? Or The Road to Kilbeggan, with my Irish endeavours?

I couldn't decide which road to take. Partly because I had begun writing a new series of books, ultimately culminating in the Drink & Music Trilogy – consisting of *Malts & Whisky* (part 1), *Bourbon & Blues* (part 2) and *Rum & Reggae* (part 3). In part two I had already used a lot of 'American stuff'. For the Dutch magazine *Whisky Passion*, I'd done a whole series about Irish distilleries. And leaving Scotland entirely out of a new book didn't strike me as a good idea altogether. After all Scottish single malts are the red thread in my life and publications.

The other reason I postponed writing a sequel had to do with the fact that the international whisky industry assigned The Whisky Couple more and more tailor-made publications, so the whole project ended up on the back burner.

I wanted to respond to the ever-growing requests from my readers, so I started to develop a concept for *Still Stories* in my head. As always, when I am ready to begin with a new book, I consult some close friends who are not afraid to give clear, sharp and honest feedback. 'Tell stories, people like that', they emphasised, 'so many books have been written about taste, smell and expression.' I could live with that. After all, telling stories is in my genes.

Playing with the concept of storytelling I suddenly saw the title of the new book in front of me, as a possible new series, and a double entendre as well. In a way this first tome of *Still Stories* is a continuation on The Road (to Craigellachie), albeit that I chose a somewhat different approach. Where I wrote *The Road* as two story lines that intertwine at the end of the book, for *Still Stories* I connect a series of events that do not necessarily follow each other chronologically. Some stories have previously appeared in other publications. The period in which they happened is shorter too, only a decade as opposed to the 30 years time span in *The Road*. Also in many of the stories, Becky is my constant travelling companion. And I can tell you, it is even more fun on The Road.

I hope you enjoy this ditty. In the meantime I'll start thinking about *Still Stories II*. Promise!

Hans Offringa

Tennessee, and then ... Kentucky

Scotch Single Malt is my first love, but Bourbon is my mistress. I met her in 1974, in an Irish pub in The Netherlands, in the guise of Four Roses Kentucky Straight Bourbon. Many meetings with bourbon siblings followed in Amsterdam, through the mid 1980s when I worked in the Dutch capital as a copywriter and media developer.

In my time off I could often be found in whisky bar L&B, in the Korte Leidse Dwarsstraat, where I must have consumed many a Turkey and a Rose, the liquid versions of the creatures of course. I didn't work in the western part of The Netherlands for long. I enjoyed my job but life was too fast paced. After two years I moved back to the city where I grew up in the east, Zwolle, close to the German border. I continued working as a copywriter at a local advertising company.

Around that time I met Jack Daniel's Tennessee Sour Mash Whiskey and began a correspondence with the then-president of the company, a Mr David Mahanes. In 1985 I received a letter from him in which he invited me to come and visit the distillery in Lynchburg, Tennessee. That's a story I already wrote down in *The Road to Craigellachie*, so I won't elaborate on that one.

I could not immediately accept the invitation. At the time I did not have the means to finance such a trip. Starting in 1994, my work as a media consultant finally brought me to the USA, especially to Los Angeles, Las Vegas and San Francisco. Not exactly neighbours of the southern states of Tennessee and Kentucky. It would take another decade before I finally was able to visit Jack Daniel's and, in its wake, Four Roses Distillery.

The road to these true whiskey states led via Charleston, South Carolina, where I had begun consulting for an American publishing company in 2001. After having studied a detailed map of the Southern States, I estimated that a trip to Jack would take me a good eight hours on the road, adding five to six hours from there to get to Four Roses. However, work with my American business partners took so much time that making such a trip wasn't feasible in the foreseeable future. I did bring Mr Mahanes written invitation from 1985 with me. After all, one never knows whom one is going to meet, eventually.

After commuting between Europe and the USA for some years, I met Becky in Charleston. It was love at first sight and it didn't take long before I proposed to her. Luckily she said 'yes' immediately and we scheduled a wedding date. Then I suggested we would go on our honeymoon to....Tennessee and, maybe too, Kentucky! My soon-to-be spouse rejected the idea instantly. Getting to know me a bit, she realised that this would turn into business travel within minutes and the whole idea of a honeymoon would disappear at the site of the first still. In the end we decided to travel to Egypt and climb Mount Sinai, but that is a different story, for a different book.

I wasn't disappointed and soon made other travelling plans. First we flew to Scotland where I introduced Becky to my unforgettable Scottish faither Bill Ross († 2009) and his wife Ulla, as well as various Scottish whisky friends and colleagues. They soon found out that Becky is an excellent taster in her own right, a real natural. She enjoyed being immersed in the whisky realm, so after our return to Charleston I boldly suggested we visit Jack and Four Roses before we were to be married. About Jack, Becky was enthusiastic immediately, but Four Roses made her make a funny face. 'Four Roses, Hans? You must be kidding! That's rotgut, for the homeless.'

I totally disagreed with her and tried every trick from my

extensive book to convince her, assisted by some online research and a few phone calls with colleagues. In the end she succumbed half-heartedly after having heard my story that where Four Roses might be a cheap blended whiskey in the USA, in Europe and Japan the brand was known as a delicious Straight Bourbon. They didn't have anything in common, except the brand name. And so we planned my first trip to Tennessee and Kentucky.

On Friday 19 May 2006, three weeks before our marriage in Charleston that would take place on Folly Beach, and more than 20 years after having received an invitation from the president of Jack Daniel's, we arrived in Lynchburg, TN. We solemnly entered the visitor centre and walked up to the receptionist, to whom I presented the long-kept letter, saying: 'I have to apologise for reacting rather late on it, but I was too busy to come earlier.'

When reading the letter, she was flabbergasted and called her manager. He loved the fact I'd kept the letter for so long and took us to the Squire Room where we were inaugurated as 'Tennessee Squires' on the spot. His secretary copied Mahanes' letter, which copy is still kept at the distillery. In years to come we would regularly return and have made friends for life in Lynchburg.

Three days after our initial visit to Jack, we parked our car in front of the Four Roses Distillery in Lawrenceburg, KY. Thanks to an introductory letter sent by Pernod Ricard NL, the official importer of Four Roses in The Netherlands, we were received as true VIPs. At first Becky had her qualms about the quality of this whiskey, but her doubts melted like snow in the sun when Jim Rutledge, Brent Elliot and Jota Tanaka, respectively master distiller, assistant master distiller and QA Director at the time, presented us with a series of samples. Jim took time to explain the story behind the cheap blend with the poor reputation in the USA and the beautiful bourbons in Europe and Japan. 'It is a true story', he added, 'but I am busy rebuilding Four Roses as a quality brand in our own country.'

Well, he did manage to do so, introducing the single barrel and small batch versions, which would in years to come win many medals. Years later Jim, who became a dear friend, contributed to *Bourbon & Blues* and was one of the people in the Kentucky Distillers Association who put in a request to the governor to name me a Kentucky Colonel. It was worth the long wait to come to this part of the world! At the time of writing Four Roses Yellow Label, the bourbon about which Becky and I had one of our spare serious disagreements, is also recognised as a quality product. Jim has retired and Brent Elliot has taken his place. Jota Tanaka now works as master blender at Fuji Gotemba distillery (both distilleries are owned by the Japanese drinks company Kirin).

We ended up spending a whole week in Kentucky and consequently visited a series of other bourbon distilleries among which Wild Turkey, Maker's Mark, Jim Beam, Heaven Hill, Buffalo Trace and Woodford Reserve. On the way back to Charleston we 'grabbed' that other Tennessee distillery, George Dickel in Tullahoma. Stories about those visits would later appear in various newspapers, magazines and of course, in *Bourbon & Blues*. The American edition was appropriately launched at Four Roses Distillery in 2011, during the Kentucky Bourbon Festival.

Naturally we brought a piece of Tennessee and Kentucky back home to The Netherlands. One of the first people who asked us to do a bourbon tasting in the NL, framed with story telling, was Leon Elshoff of L&B, my old whisky stomping ground in Amsterdam. For me, that is all about Conceptual Continuity! From that moment we have considered it a special mission to promote Bourbon and Tennessee Whiskey in Europe, next to Scotch and Irish. Nowadays, Jack Daniel's and Four Roses regularly appear in a line up when we are asked to do a master class on American whiskeys. I've also been touring through The Netherlands with two blues musicians for five years, them playing blues tunes, me telling bourbon and blues stories live on stage. We are called 'the Small Batch' and maybe we will show up some time in other parts of the world. See you then!

Whiskey in General

Once The Whisky Couple was invited to a party in honour of Robert E. Lee's birthday. Clad in full highland attire we gathered at the Confederate Home in Charleston, SC and celebrated the life and times of that great Southern gentleman and excellent military commander. While standing on the porch, I engaged in a lively conversation with Mr Frank G. Cain. When we toasted the General with the appropriate drink, my companion told me that Lee had been very fond of whiskey and suggested I dedicate an article in the *Charleston Mercury* (a newspaper for which we've been writing since 2007) to 'general issues regarding whiskey'.

Back home I googled 'Lee and whiskey' and up popped his famous quote: 'I like whiskey. I always did, and that is why I never use it.' With a quote like that you can't get very far when writing about the drink in general(s), so it made me think about another general, notorious for his heavy drinking, but very successful in battle. It made Abraham Lincoln utter during a Cabinet meeting in 1864: 'If I knew what brand of whiskey he drinks, I would send a barrel or so to some other generals.' Lincoln, of course, was referring to Ulysses Grant. His name doesn't bring happy memories to every Southerner, so I decided not to delve into his life. However he did make it to President, and that train of thought led me to George Washington.That famous military commander and the first President of the USA also had a finger in the whiskey pie.

'A distillery is a business I am entirely unacquainted with, but from your knowledge of it and from the confidence you have in the profit to be derived from the establishment, I am disposed to enter upon one.' These were the words

George Washington wrote to his plantation manager James Anderson in June 1797.

Anderson came from Scotland and that says it all. Being a farmer looking for a more prosperous life he emigrated from Inverkeithing and took his distilling knowledge with him. After gaining the consent of his employer, he set to work immediately. It didn't take long before Washington profited from the Scot's knowledge and zeal. Just two years later, five pot stills at Mount Vernon Estate produced 11,000 gallons – making a profit of $ 7,500, a small fortune at the time.

George Washington developed the habit of keeping a diary and was a fervent writer of letters. Thanks to those practices, many facts are known about his life, his work and his way of thinking. He was born on February 22, 1732, on his father's plantation in Pope's Creek, Westmoreland County, Virginia. Age three he moved with his parents and siblings to Little Hunting Creek Plantation, later to be renamed Mount Vernon. When 11 he lost his father and George had to take care of the plantation and therefore was not able to enjoy a formal education. In 1748 he became land surveyor thanks to the neighbours of his older brother Lawrence. When he visited Barbados in 1751, Washington came in contact with military life. A year later Lawrence died and left Mount Vernon to his younger brother, as well as his place in the Virginia Militia. Soon George would be involved in the conflicts with the French. He became so successful as a soldier that he was appointed supreme commander of the Virginian army in 1755. When peace returned four years later, at the age of 27 he married a rich widow and withdrew from public and military life on his plantation. From 1759 to 1775 he lived the life of the landed gentry and enjoyed it. Then he became politically active, earning a seat in the Continental Congress in 1774.

When the Revolutionary War started in 1776 his peaceful

life came to an abrupt end. Washington returned to the army and after five years of uninterrupted fighting with the English he accepted commander Cornwallis' surrender of the British Army on 19 October 1781. He returned to his beloved Mount Vernon, but stayed politically active. In 1785 he would be instrumental in establishing the American Constitution. When it passed in 1787, for the first time in history presidential elections were held in the young Federation. Washington won all votes unanimously, an occurrence that has not been repeated by any other American president. He served two terms from 1789 till 1797, after which time he returned to Mount Vernon again, where he learned to distil at the age of 65.

Although not a heavy imbiber himself, he was a big proponent of drinking in the army. In 1777 he had instructed the procurement officer of the Continental Army 'there should always be enough whiskey to give moderate portions to the troops ... especially when they have to march on hot or cold weather, and have to make their camp in the wet cold ... it is so essential that we cannot do without.'

Washington was not only a successful military commander and politician, but also a sound businessman and an enlightened landowner. He educated his slaves in various professions, such as shoemaker, blacksmith, mason and... distiller, with the purpose that, when the slaves would be free men, they could earn a living. When a politician he once learned a valuable lesson about whiskey. In the middle of the 18th century it was common to 'buy' votes by offering free whiskey to the common people, just before the elections started. The one time Washington skipped that custom he immediately lost. It wouldn't happen to him a second time. Whiskey delivered votes and money.

Unfortunately he only enjoyed his new distilling venture for two years. On 14 December 1799 the first President of the United States died of pneumonia. His last words were: 'I die hard, but I am not afraid to go.' The distillery was kept alive, albeit stumbling and failing. Washington's nephew Lawrence Lewis was named the official heir. James Anderson left the estate and that must have been a severe loss to the new owner. In 1808 the stills were fired for the last time. The buildings were not maintained and in 1814 they burnt to the ground. It seemed to be the end of the distillery. Or not?

181 years later a small miracle happened. In 1995 a plan was developed to research the possible resurrection of the 18th century distillery. Between 1997 and 1998 the entire location was charted thoroughly and from 1999 until 2002 exhaustive excavations took place. It took considerable time to get the necessary permits, but in 2005 the rebuilding started, thanks to a 1.2 million dollar donation by the Distilled Spirits Council of the United States (DISCUS). On 27 September 2006 HRH Prince Andrew reopened the distillery. A DISCUS spokesman remarked at the occasion: 'This is an incredible possibility for America to restore the heritage of distillation lost during Prohibition.'

Today the distillery is part of Mount Vernon Estate. The many visitors all want to see the home of George Washington with their own eyes. DISCUS uses Mount Vernon as the starting place of the American Whiskey Trail. A small amount of whiskey was distilled exclusively for the opening festivities, following the recipe that would have been used by Washington and Anderson two centuries ago. The copper pot still is an exact replica of an 18th century still that was found and confiscated by the police after a raid at a local moonshiner's place. The manufacturing year on the still reads 1787 but it isn't clear whether the President ever used it.

The entirely reconstructed distillery is the only one in the USA that shows from start to finish how whiskey would have been made in the 18th century. Beside the stone and wooden still house one can see Washington's old water mill, also restored to its former splendour. It supplies the distillery with milled grain. Whiskey is only made in very small quantities for special events. The stillman is dressed in traditional clothing and the whiskey is only sold on the premises. The barrels for aging are copies of 19th century 10-gallon casks. George Washington is remembered daily with his portrait on the dollar bill, but also reclaims his rightful position in American whiskey history.

A Family Affair

I am sitting in an old barn somewhere between Penfield and Armstrong, Illinois. It is part of a farm. While I write this the farmer who owns the property is working behind me, restoring an old piano. He retired a few years ago and leases his 880 acres to a young farmer who continues to grow corn, wheat, oats and soybeans in this soil. The retired farmer's name is John Dewey. His great-great-grandfather purchased lands in this area somewhere in the 1800s and the farm has been handed down the generations since. John Dewey is married to Marilyn Lovett. They have one son, Andrew, who moved away some years ago and currently lives near Springfield, Illinois. He wasn't interested in farming, so the buck stops here.

For many years John has been fascinated with player pianos and he is considered an expert in this field. His being invited as a speaker to many conferences testifies to that. Steinway & Sons recommends him for restoring their action frames. When I look around, and it is really in the proverbial middle-of-nowhere, it is amazing to be surrounded by half dismantled pianos, keys, all kinds of parts that I cannot immediately name properly, which will find their place in a restored piano sometime.

About 10 miles further up the road stands an awkwardly shaped wooden house with a very pointed roof. According to John the previous owner built the house and then managed to get a huge grand piano on the top floor. When he sold the house to the current inhabitant, he just left it there. John was summoned for advice, but couldn't figure out how on earth the huge instrument had gotten there. I suggested the house might have been built around it, but he was sure this was not the case. The new owner really wanted to get rid of it and offered it to the farmer-turned-fulltime-piano-restorer. John took one more look at the backbreaking piece of musical furniture and supplied the owner with a single word of advice, 'Sledgehammer.' Some things simply cannot be saved for posterity.

We came here for a family visit, since Marilyn is the younger sister of Becky's father. It also gave me the opportunity to talk with a man from a long lineage of farmers. The Deweys certainly belong to one of the first settlers in this area. Originally they came from England.

Together with Missouri, Kansas, Iowa, Indiana and Wisconsin, Illinois is one of the primary states that supply the Kentucky bourbon distillers with corn and wheat. So here is your angle on whiskey. One branch of my family back in Friesland farms too, and I used to spend holidays there, playing with my cousins in the haystacks and such. However, they are dairy farmers, so I didn't have an opportunity to learn about growing crops at that place. Now I sit down with Uncle John and ask him questions about growing corn. I want to know what things might jeopardise the harvest. Patiently he answers questions from a city boy and I get acquainted with rootworm, black soil that kills the turkeys, deer that came from the northwest and can cause damage to the fields, coyotes that are such avid scavengers that they caused the fox to disappear from this region – simply because he couldn't compete for food anymore.

I learn about the electrical fences that are meant to protect the semi-free-range turkeys and chickens from predators. Uncle John tells a story about a huge owl that caught a turkey and whilst eating it for supper, stumbled and managed to touch the electrical fence with the turkey. The latter being a fine conductor, he literally zapped the owl post-mortem. So much for Illinois Fried Turkey.

This anecdote brings me to a question about the feathered

beasties. I want to know how they are slaughtered. Picture an inverted traffic cone like the ones used during road repairs. There is a hole in the pointed end and the turkey is put in the cone, its head sticking out. Then the farmer slits its throat. The cone prevents the bird from flapping wildly around and bruising the meat. It gives me an entirely new meaning for the word cone-head. I shrug, my lively imagination running wild, envisioning a whole field of tightly coned turkeys waiting to meet their end. I prefer the liquid variety known as Wild Turkey.

But back to the corn. It doesn't arrive easily in your bourbon. After it is sown, ideally by the first of May, it has to battle with various natural enemies before it can be harvested. Depending on the weather conditions, the harvesting season can stretch out from late August up until Christmas. Bugs, fungi, mould are the primary enemies. The rootworm eats up the roots, whereas the corn borer, honouring its name, bores holes in the stalks, which will become weak and be destroyed in a strong wind. Remarkably enough another insect, a little wasp imported from Europe, is used to battle the corn borer. The little wasp runs up and down the stalk, tapping it like a woodpecker and by listening to the echo knows where the corn borer is. It then eats the little critter. Southerly winds take the corn borer moths to Illinois. So, for the farmers over here, the northern wind is their friend. When the summer is very humid and warm (not hot, but warm) the corn might suffer from various fungi. Tornados don't do too much damage, but can hit small pockets of grains, representing less than 0.1 percent of the entire area. Sometimes the weather can be cruel. In the early 2000s Uncle John experienced a micro burst. It is a natural phenomenon that occurs when a cold and warm front collide. The result is a downdraft – a straight fierce wind that can reach a velocity of 140 miles an hour. It hit Uncle John's property and caused more than $50,000 in damage, ruining part of the crops and the machine shed, where the wind blew off the siding and cracked the roof. This is thankfully a rather rare event.

Soybeans are sown in mid-May and harvested about the same time as the corn. The oats go into the soil in March and are full-grown in summer. Uncle John targets the 4th of July as the main day to start harvesting. Wheat is sown in October and harvested together with the oats; hence it is called winter wheat.

Uncle John's property is slightly above the average acreage in this part of the USA. The yearly harvest is usually 60 to 70,000 bushels* of corn, about 18,000 bushels of soybeans, 6,000 bushels of wheat and 500 of oats. The latter is primarily used for chicken feed.

It is rather difficult to give an estimate of how much of Uncle John's corn ends up in bourbon, since the crops are sold to a grain processing company, but some of it will end up in alcoholic beverages. Theoretically the Dewey 70,000 bushels of corn could lead a second life as 196,000 gallons** of ethanol. But I'd like to believe that it is going into some of America's fine whiskeys instead, making our next glass of bourbon a family affair.

---

* 1 bushel = 25.4 kilo
** 1 gallon = 3.78 litre

No Ice(land) in My Whisky

In 2010 Becky and I received an e-mail invitation from a Canadian gentleman who presented himself as a marketing executive of a management consulting agency. That is not my line of business, but reading the email I quickly grasped what the man and I shared in common: a sincere love of the drink called whisk(e)y. Said man, whom we will call Mr Canada for now, referred to his website. At the time I was in Charleston, working on the manuscript of *Bourbon & Blues*, the sequel to *Whisky & Jazz*, hence I was living in the same time zone as Mr Canada, based in Quebec.

Wanting to know more about his invitation and our joint fascination, I set up a Skype conversation with him. Soon it became clear to me that he was seriously planning to set up an international whisky competition – the umpteenth one, was my first reaction. However, by listening to him explaining the way he would organise the tasting, I became more interested and over the next week we frequently Skyped. Mr Canada is not only fascinated by whisky but also by social media. He'd invited several people to become judges at his planned competition that would take place in Chicago. The idea was to broadcast the event on the web, using Facebook, YouTube, Twitter, Linked-in, Hyves, live video streams, email and any other means of digital communication.

Having spent part of my professional career in digital media, I was immediately interested in his idea, which had the potential to distinguish itself from previous whisky competitions. The event being held in Chicago gave me another impetus. I could visit a few blues clubs, doing additional research for *Bourbon & Blues*. So, we said yes and two weeks later left Charleston for Europe. Soon the official dates of the whisky competition were made known to us – April 8 -10,

with ample time to enjoy the city. It meant we would have to fly back to the USA only a month after we'd returned to our home in The Netherlands, but what the heck. This looked like a very interesting opportunity to combine social media with my favourite drink. When I mentioned the event in an email to our intrepid publisher and editor-in-chief Charles Waring, he immediately contacted an independent PR agent working and living partly in Charleston, partly in New York City. He asked her to set up a few book signings for *Whisky & Jazz* in the Big Apple and planned it immediately after our Chicago gig. So far, so good.

The Whisky Competition looked fine, as far as the social media component was concerned, as well as the international composition of the jury. Mr Canada had chosen a Scotsman, a Canadian, a Belgian, a Dutchman, an Indian gentleman and two Americans. Unfortunately the man from India did not show up and the Scot appeared to be only 20 years old. Becky found this out during the welcome dinner preceding the competition. She noticed he only drank Coke and asked if he disliked wine. 'Legally I am I am not allowed to drink alcohol in the USA', was the short answer. When she told me later in our hotel room, I was appalled and astonished. 'Yes', Becky continued, 'he agreed to come for the free trip to Chicago and thought he would just see what happened'.

The next day my astonishment grew even larger. Mr Canada had only managed to acquire 50 different entries, mainly Scotch single malts and he'd divided them into more than 12 (!) categories. I took him apart and told him this event hardly deserved the adjective International. 'And something else. One of your jury members is younger than 21!' He responded rather irritably that he did not really care and I should not create problems. 'Do you realise that this hotel can lose its licence? When this gets around, you can get out of the country via your embassy, but the two American

judges, one of them my wife, may enter into prison for this.'
Mr Canada wanted to ignore my arguments and made a ges-
ture with his hands as if he wanted to wave this away like
a mosquito who just bit him, until I slightly raised my voice
and continued: 'OK, then we are out right now', and assembled our laptops and notebooks. Mr Canada panicked slightly and I offered him a way out. I would talk to the young
Scotsman, offering him a role as 'non-participating observ-
er', which the latter gladly accepted. 'And I do not want to
see him drinking any alcoholic beverage', I added. In a way it
was a shame, since in Scotland he would have been allowed
to be a participating judge.

During one of the intervals I got into an animated discussion with the discarded judge and among other things
told him about International Whisky Day (IWD), a non-profit
initiative we undertook in 2009 in memory of the legendary beer and whisky writer Michael Jackson who had suddenly and unexpectedly died in 2007 as a consequence of
Parkinson's Disease. IWD was supported by many people
in the whisky industry and raised money for the Parkinson
Foundation. The young Scotsman loved the story. In 2011
he shamelessly copied our initiative with the commercially
based World Whisky Day and even had the audacity to first
deny any knowledge of our initiative. Many people in the
industry were not amused. I chose not to react, other than
mentioning tongue-in-cheek on social media that 'imitation
is the sincerest form of flattery that mediocrity can pay to
greatness', which is borrowing in itself (I loaned the quote
from Oscar Wilde).

But let's turn back to that Chicago event in the spring
of 2010. Due to the meagre number of participating whiskies and whiskeys, in between the sampling sessions there
was ample time to explore Chicago. Among other places we
visited the Art Institute, took in the view of the city from

the Hancock Tower, strolled the Navy Pier and visited Buddy Guy's Blues Legends club. There we enjoyed the Lonnie Brooks Band and encountered living legend Bruce Iglauer, founder of Alligator Records and discoverer of Hounddog Taylor, among many other famous blues musicians.

After five days in the Windy City we transferred to NYC, where the PR lady had set up book signings with Park Avenue Wine & Liquor – one of the most famous whisky retailers in the world – and Union Square Liquors at the eponymous square. The latter is a wine and spirits shop that is wonderfully designed to hold events in their back room. The proprietor had contracted a jazz combo and his most valued customers came streaming in. All whisky importers of the brands mentioned in *Whisky & Jazz* had their own stands. The people could sample and listen at the same time and talk with us about the book. Among them was Peter Silver, the famous jazz-dentist of NYC and one of the revered Malt Maniacs, of which there are only 24 in the world. They have taken tasting to the extreme and are considered an influential group in the world of whisky. Mr Silver loved the combination of music and malt, and when I told him I'd done another whisky book (*The Legend of Laphroaig*) with a Dutch colleague of his, his evening only got better.

The PR lady hired by the Charleston Mercury, whom we met for the first time, turned out to be a real gem and suggested some interesting things for us to do when off duty. For me, only having been there once for two days, it was an opportunity to get to know NYC a tiny bit better. High on my agenda was the John Lennon Memorial in Central Park. Close to the Imagine mosaic, I put in my earbuds, turned on my iPod and listened to a unique recording of Lennon and Frank Zappa, taken on 6 June 1971 in the Fillmore East Theatre in the Village. On YouTube you may still find a little video about that event. Try http://www.youtube.com/

watch?v=ORFU3AD3N_Y. The song can also be found on the FZ double album *Playground Psychotics*. Afterwards we ventured to the Metropolitan Museum. Becky paints in her free time, so we paid extra attention to the paintings displayed. We stayed in a nice apartment in the upper West side, with shops, restaurants and bars nearby. We thoroughly enjoyed the city for a few days, albeit it that my heart lies in the southeast, in Charleston, and that will be forever.

The day we were to fly back, we got up rather early and checked the website to confirm our flight was on time. The evening before, we'd heard sombre stories in the pub across from our temporary dwelling about a volcano in Iceland… however, the airline website informed us there were no delays so we decided to go to JFK. Then, disaster struck. Deep was our disappointment when upon arrival we were confronted with the words 'flight cancelled'. We were directed to a line of people and eventually summoned to the desk of a tired looking airline employee. After having shown him our itinerary he looked at us like a sad dog. 'I can get you on a flight two weeks from now,' he sighed, already anticipating verbal abuse. I can be a bit high strung in such situations so I usually leave this kind of thing in the capable hands of Becky, who has far more empathy and patience.

Kindly she explained to the man that we had to catch a ferry to Scotland from Europe in eight days and it would be impossible to wait that long for a new flight. The man was susceptible to her charm. When Becky suggested he might book us on a partner airline, his eyes lit up, his fingers hit the keyboard and within 35 seconds a broad smile appeared on his stubbled face. 'What about in a week? I can have you flown to Munich and from there to Amsterdam!' A quick calculation revealed that we would have exactly one day to change suitcases in Zwolle and then get in the car, racing to Amsterdam to catch the ferry to Newcastle.

I frowned and didn't utter a single syllable, staring into the distance, looking annoyed. 'I recommend you accept this flight. It will be gone in no time, since we have to re-schedule 19 million passengers worldwide,' the attendant said to Becky. She nodded with a sigh and he printed our temporary boarding passes. 'Your husband doesn't respond. He's okay?' the attendant wanted to know. 'Leave him be,' Becky responded, 'he doesn't like Iceland in his whisky.'

***

So, there we were, stuck in NYC, because of a tiny volcano on an island with no more than roughly 300,000 inhabitants. At first I was irritated, but gradually a feeling of humility overcame me. Having travelled the greater part of the world and only experiencing some lost luggage and a missed connection once in a while, I suddenly realised that with all we can achieve today, nature only has to rear its head a bit and we are lost. Utterly lost. 19 million people displaced and waiting to be rescheduled in the next few weeks by soon overworked airline employees.

I needed a drink, a stiff one. When we had secured our flight with Lufthansa for the next week we returned to the city, headed for a bar and ordered a Wild Turkey 101, with that extra bite of rye I like so much when I feel fatigued. At the bar we made a game plan what to do. First we checked some hotel prices on the web. It was remarkable how quickly the hospitality branch responded to the worldwide air passenger constipation with an astonishing increase in hotel room rates, knowing that beggars can't be choosers. The Whisky Couple is not known for panicking in ad hoc situations and we decided to call Becky's other aunt from the Lovett side of the family, Kathy, who lives with her husband Rudy Peterson in Schenectady, New York, famous for being the cradle of General Electric. Luckily the Petersens were home, since they are avid travellers themselves, with a fondness for the lesser-known parts of the world.

They were delighted to have us for a week and suggested we take the Amtrak to Albany where they would pick us up from the train station. Thanks to internet and the wireless world, we quickly found out we could get a train the same day. While Becky was securing tickets I twittered, facebooked and blogged on various whisky websites that we were stuck, and I sent some emails to inform business clients that I could not make our appointments for the coming week.

It is amazing how rapidly people respond in the online social media world. A distant cousin in Boston, MA, offered us a place at his holiday home in Cape Cod within two minutes after I updated my Facebook page. A business contact in The Netherlands asked if I could bring him a bottle of Johnnie Walker Double Black, an extra peated expression of this famous blended Scotch – then only available at JFK and five other airports all located in the middle and far East. Said man forgot to show empathy with our situation as he was so focused on his whisky. So much for compassion! My cousin Elisabeth Offringa Baxendale, living in Atlanta, let me know instantly that we were welcome at a moment's notice, as a counterbalance to the Johnnie Walker fan's reaction.

Meanwhile Becky returned from the desk with two Amtrak tickets to Albany in hand and at 7 pm we boarded the train. Actually it is a nice journey, following the course of the Hudson River upstream. Almost three hours later we were welcomed by Aunt Kathy and Uncle Rudy at the train platform and headed to their house in Schenectady.

Uncle Rudy, who knows about my passion for whisky, apologised that he could only offer me a Jack Daniel's. 'I get one bottle each year for my birthday, from my children. And it takes me the whole year to finish it. I prefer a beer instead.'

I do enjoy Jack Daniel's from time to time but that night I was more in the mood for a single malt, so I dug in my suitcase and came up with a full bottle of The Balvenie Portwood 21-year-old, a present we received for being judges at the whisky competition in Chicago two weeks earlier. This stunning and smooth single malt is the perfect nightcap. Willing to broaden his horizon with a new whisky, Uncle Rudy decided to have one, too.

Anxiously I regarded him while he took a sip. For a moment it was quiet, very quiet and then a broad smile appeared on his face, 'This is good stuff, very good stuff!' Ah, to initiate the unaware... it always gives me great pleasure. Soon after this brief exploration in the world of Scotch single malt we went to bed, exhausted by the day's unusual events. That night I dreamt about a way to use active volcanoes to fire up the pot stills in the Scottish distilleries. Unfortunately the brilliant idea I conceived in the night had totally disappeared from my mind the next morning when we were awakened by the smell of bacon and eggs coming from below. We went down to the kitchen where a full breakfast was laid out for us, with Uncle Rudy waiting with a piece of paper and a pencil in hand. He is a planner, rather a fanatic planner. Early that morning he'd drawn up one of his famous to-do-lists, an entire itinerary for the Whisky Couple, should we not know what to do with that extra week in the US.

Little did Uncle Rudy know. Since we always travel with at least one laptop, I can write and work on articles and books anywhere in the world. Apart from that I carry our total digital photo library on the hard disk. That proved to be extremely handy, since the next day I received a request from a Scottish fellow writer who needed some pictures for his next book. However, Becky suggested we take a couple of days off, to visit her 93-year-old grandmother, who happened to live in Schenectady too – that was a bonus, since we hadn't seen her since after her 90th birthday – and to take some trips through the countryside. Uncle Rudy immediately had some ideas and added them to his To-Do-List. Remembering that I 'collect' states he put Massachusetts and Vermont into the itinerary – indeed ones that I had not visited before. Not forgetting Becky he included a visit to the grave of Robert Frost, the great American poet, one of her favourites. Next was a tour of William's College museum in Massachusetts, where we saw a life-sized model of a sperm whale made entirely of felt and inspired by Melville's *Moby Dick*. In Manchester, Vermont we stopped to visit the famous Northshire Bookstore where I couldn't resist the temptation of buying a copy of a new American book on whisky, titled *The Art of Distilling Whisky and Other Spirits*. The literary aspects of our trip were not forgotten.

Every day upon our return I took a sip of Jack Daniel's, breaking all the records in the Petersen household regarding how long/short a bottle of the famous Tennessee whiskey could be kept before being emptied. In the evening Aunt Kathy showed us amazing pictures of their travels to Alaska, Antarctica and (what was somewhat ironic, all things considered) Iceland. How much ice can one take with one's whiskey…

So in the end our forced encounter with the volcanic ashes turned into an extended family visit that we thoroughly enjoyed. And on the side I was able to convert a Jack Daniel's fan into an admirer of single malt whisky. When we finally left to get the train to JFK a week later, I left the Balvenie on the counter, just to convey an implicit message to Uncle Rudy's boys.

WH

PARK AVEN

SCOTCH... BOURBONS & RYES! UH MY!

Whisky & Jazz

PARK AVENUE
SHOP BOOK SI...
AND WHISKY TA...

Whisky
& Jazz

Big Whisky, Big Apple

The USA is more than Kentucky and Bourbon, or Tennessee and Jack Daniel. One enjoys a single malt in this country, too, especially in the big cities. I was to find that out again when I received an invitation to travel to New York with a select group of lifestyle journalists, to come and taste a vintage whisky. A perfect opportunity to return to the Big Apple and maintain contacts, since it had been a few years ago since we'd been in Manhattan to do book signings for *Whisky & Jazz*. And even better, to taste a very rare vintage single malt.

The main goal of the short visit to the US was the launch of an exclusive 50-year-old Highland Park at the famous Brandy Library, 25 North Moore St, in the trendy Tribeca neighbourhood. Among the little group were editors of the Dutch editions of *Elle Food*, *Playboy* and *Esquire*, the then-brand manager in The Netherlands, a formidable lady called Ilja Schouten and a young promising female photographer by the name of Kelly Vanderdussen. It was a bit of a change of scenery for me, because usually Becky accompanies me on my foreign trips. However, this time she stayed at home, tied to her desk, dealing with a strict deadline for editing a new large English whisky publication we were to launch in a few months.

After an uneventful flight we arrived at JFK and were collected by a chauffeur in a pitch black minivan, complete with blinding windows that allowed looking outside but prevented people peering inside. This vehicle would take us around NYC for the coming three days. Within the hour we parked in front of our hotel on Madison Avenue, not far from the famous stadium where Rod Stewart would perform two days later.

An American colleague of Ilja welcomed us and invited us for a special dinner in a cosy and hip restaurant across the street. The next day was reserved for visits to a few liquor stores, among which Park Avenue and Union Square Spirits and Wine, old acquaintances from the Whisky & Jazz Sessions. Lunch took place at another trendy restaurant and then we started warming up for the launch and tasting of the HP 50. Literally warming up, since the driver had been given the afternoon off since the weather in the Big Apple was very agreeable and perfect for a stroll.

After having walked among skyscrapers for half an hour, we arrived at the Brandy Library and received a cordial welcome. To calibrate the palate we were all presented with a flight of 18, 25, 30 and 40-year-old HP, vintages I was lucky to have tasted before, but never head-to-head. I thoroughly enjoyed revisiting these drams and realised again how excellent a single malt Highland Park is, every expression adding its own quality to the range. They all taste good, no matter in what order you savour them. Martin Daraz, the American HP ambassador, guided us, filled with knowledge, in a fierce tempo through the tasting and then the highlight of the day was presented – a Highland Park of half a century old, about my age at the time. We watched in awe when the beautiful packaging was revealed and everyone present received a thimbleful, measure wise, of the precious amber liquid in their glasses. A serene calm befell the small band of scribblers, who were then joined by a foursome of well-known whisky aficionado's – well-known in New York that is – recruited from Mighty Martin's network.

I've had the opportunity to taste very old whiskies before and that is not always a pleasure. Not every dram can take the wood for a long period and it's always a surprise what comes out of the cask, or barrel if you prefer. Well, Highland Park, just as its stable mate The Macallan, has a reputation with old vintages and can take the oak very well. We already noticed in the previous flight, where the 30-year-old turned out to be the group's favourite. But what would happen with another 20 years in the cask?

Slowly I turned the glass and admired the deep mahogany colour of the liquid inside. My nose decided to live its own life and carefully sniffed the contents. Immediately a distinctive spicy note emerged, slowly developing into a very complex mixture of herbs and spices, with nutmeg and cloves at the fore. Bottled at 44.8% ABV this HP 50 did not need any water, at least for me. The taste was incredibly smooth for a whisky that age. The finish was long and warming, a little tight, but that may be expected after such a long stay in oak wood. It didn't do the impression of the whisky any harm. On the contrary, it was a grand finale.

What to do after such a royal dram? During the dinner afterwards in one of the better-known steakhouses in Manhattan, I did not dare to order a glass of whisky anymore. I was just happily satisfied and perfectly content with a glass of beer accompanying my food. A few hours later we were back at the hotel, but I did not go in yet. There was other business to be taken care of – important business – such as buying an Apple in the Big Apple !

On 5th Avenue, a 20 minute walk from our hotel, stands a futuristic Apple Store, a gigantic glass cube in which a spiral staircase winds its way down under the pavement to the actual store. Our photographer Kelly and I were intent on purchasing the (then) brand new iPad-2 and had tried during the day, in vain. Sold out! But... around 12 at night new stock would have arrived. We thought it pretty cool to wander in Manhattan around midnight and score a useful tool (according to Hans) / a fancy gadget (according to Becky), so we went to the store for the second time in 24 hours. Again, no luck. There were too few for the enormous queue of people already formed in front of us. Tired and disappointed we walked back to the hotel – no iPad in New York for us.

The next morning, after breakfast, we were offered the chance to meet the designer of the HP 50 packaging – Maeve Gillies, a Scottish lady living in New York, where she has her own gallery. Maeve is a jewellery designer originally who was approached to design a stunning silver casing around the bottle and its wooden box. An appropriate choice, since both whisky and woman come from the Orkney Islands in the North of Scotland. After an extensive interview for a Dutch whisky magazine, I followed our companions to Weather Up for a genuine cocktail workshop, conducted by owner Richard Boccato and his sidekick Valentino Gonzales. They explained how to make a proper cocktail. One of the tastiest in my book was a special Orcadian cocktail with fresh lime, honey syrup, ginger syrup from freshly pressed ginger, Highland Park 12, topped with its 18 year old sibling, poured over a square block of ice, made in the cellar with the use of a 6,000 dollar ice machine. Then we were asked if we wanted to make our own concoctions. I volunteered and, guided by maestro Richard himself, managed to make a Manhattan in Manhattan. To honour our host Ilja, I dedicated the drink to her, adding a tiny bit of Highland Park to the recipe.

Afterwards we had time to wander through Soho for a good hour. Knowing from previous visits that another Apple store was nearby, I went there straightaway, testing my luck for the third time. Lo and behold, they had two iPads in store. I instantly bought one and proudly showed it to my companions on Union Square.

Our last day in NYC was celebrated with a pub crawl. Two bars specifically I'd like to recommend: Highlands in the West Village and Mary Queen of Scots in the Lower Eastside. The owner successfully managed to create an old world atmosphere reminiscent of Scotland. It was the perfect end to a great trip and befitting our original goal: the presentation and tasting of a Big Whisky in the Big Apple. Highland Park and New York form an excellent cocktail.

Flying back to Europe, high in the sky above the Atlantic, I thoroughly enjoyed writing some tasting notes, the first ones on my iPad2!

Lord of the Drams

Of the big five whisky nations in the world, Canada is the most overlooked one. Where one can find excellent books on American, Scottish, Irish and Japanese whisky, books on the Canadian version are obscure and rare. In books that deal with whiskies worldwide, Canada usually gets just a few pages, where the others are presented with much more text and photography. I tend to ignore this type of whisky, since it is generally too sweet and perfumed for my taste. Actually, I have never written a piece about Canadian whisky before, so here is a premiere. All this neglect doesn't mean the Canadians don't know how to make and sell whisky. They just spell it different than the Americans!

A gentleman called Thomas Molson is credited with the start of Canada's whisky distilling history. Records show he founded the first whisky distillery in Montreal, Canada in 1821. Before that, distilling took place primarily in the coastal regions, but the main product was rum made from imported Caribbean molasses. This rum was largely exported, being at the time the favourite drink among sailors – legitimate and otherwise. Pirate stories have an abundance of rum drinking scoundrels and their likes. But by 1880 the Canadian whisky industry had matured into an adult with various distilleries, among which Gooderham, Worts, Seagram's, Hiram Walker and Corby's, dispersed over the vast country. Since Canada was not hit by Prohibition in the way its southern neighbour was, the industry expanded, not in the least because of that same Prohibition. Millions of cases were smuggled into the USA between 1920 and 1933. And that's one of the reasons why many Americans still drink Canadian whisky today. Sometimes they even mistakenly consider a Canadian whisky to be an American bourbon.

Today Canada has nine major players, not counting micro-distilleries. From west to east they are known as Highwood (Calgary, Alberta), Alberta (Calgary, Alberta), Black Velvet (Lethbridge, Alberta), Gimli (Gimli, Manitoba), Canadian Mist (Collingwood, Ontario), Hiram Walker (Walkerville, Ontario), Kittling Ridge (Grimsby, Ontario), Valleyfield (Salaberry-de-Valleyfield, Quebec) and Glenora (Inverness County, Nova Scotia). The latter is the only one of these to produce a single malt. Several of these distilleries have aliases: Hiram Walker is also known as Canadian Club and Walkerville. Black Velvet sometimes goes by Palliser. Valleyfield is locally referred to as Schenley. Highwood, originally Sunnyvale, purchased Potter's in 2005, which distillery was also known as Cascadia. The Canadian whisky industry, like its cousins, has had a fair share of takeovers, mergers and sales. By law Canadian whisky, which is made of rye, wheat and corn, may contain a small percentage of fruit wines, an additive that is strictly forbidden in bourbon, Irish, Scottish and Japanese whisky. It gives the whisky that distinctive sweetness that many people enjoy in their dram.

Once Seagram's was a household word in the Canadian whisky industry, together with the name Samuel Bronfman. He was born in Russia on 27 February 1889. His father Yechiel was a wealthy tobacco farmer who decided to immigrate to Canada. Young Sam saw his family fall from riches to rags when his father found he could not grow tobacco in the cold northern climate. He was forced to work as a manual labourer but showed determination and courage, venturing into new enterprises like selling firewood and trading in frozen fish.

In 1903 the Bronfman family bought a hotel and Sam soon noticed that liquor was a main profit maker in this line of business. He decided to become a distributor and soon afterwards founded The Distillers Corporation in 1924, when Prohibition had already hit the USA. It is said that the Bronfmans earned tremendous amounts of money bootlegging whisky that was made legally in Canada, to Chicago and Boston.

In 1928 Bronfman acquired Seagram Distillery and that was the start of the worldwide growth of his empire. Over time Seagram's bought many distilleries and brands in Scotland, among which The Glenlivet and Chivas Regal.

Bronfman was respected and feared, not especially loved. Small by stature he was a giant in successful business practices and generous in giving. The Samuel and Saidye Bronfman Family Foundation is one of Canada's largest private granting institutions and Bronfman received The Order of Canada in 1967. His surname in Yiddish means 'liquor man,' so he could surely be nicknamed 'Lord of the Drams' in 1960s Canada, with a nod to J.R.R. Tolkien's masterpiece trilogy.

When he died in 1972 his two sons took over. The old Seagram Distillery was closed in 1992 and production transferred elsewhere. In the early 2000s Sam's grandson decided to sell Seagram's liquor division to Pernod Ricard, investing the proceeds in Vivendi, an international entertainment group. That meant the end of the Bronfmans in the whisky industry.

One of today's foremost players in Canada is Diageo, owner of the huge Gimli plant in the eponymous village which has a colourful history. The village is located on the southwest shore of Lake Winnipeg, about 40 miles north of Winnipeg.

The area was settled in 1875 by Icelanders, a large number of whom were fleeing the disaster following volcanic eruptions in their homeland. Nothing new under the sun, right? They named their first village Gimli, after the name of paradise (or land of the Gods) in Norse. Gimli still has the largest Icelandic community outside Iceland. North of Gimli, Manitoba borders the Hudson Bay and from that direction the first Vikings supposedly came to North America around the 11th and 12th century, long before Columbus, leaving their homes in Scandinavia and Iceland to cross the Atlantic.

Their Viking heritage and settlement of the area is commemorated in Gimli by large murals on the harbour seawall, as well as during the annual Icelandic Festival. And just along the road, 1.4 million barrels of spirit that will become whisky are quietly aging in 46 warehouses of the Gimli distillery.

The name Gimli reminds me of Tolkien again. Gimli, the axe-wielding dwarf who assisted the hobbit Frodo in trying to destroy the Ring in the fires of Mordor. Gimli distillery produces that famous and very popular Crown Royal, often mistaken for a bourbon in the USA. I happen to like that specific one and, because the Bronfman's no longer are present in the drinks industry, propose to 'Crown' Royal as the new Lord of the Canadian Drams.

Italian Job

The village of Rothes in the Speyside is far, far away from that south-European country shaped in the form of a boot, and well-loved by British tourists: Italy. However, there is a distinctive connection between both places. One of the five distilleries in Rothes is named Glen Grant. Founded in 1840 by two brothers, James and John Grant, it prospered from the start, slowly but surely building a name for itself as a gentle, light and restorative dram. Independent bottlers loved this light whisky and bought many casks over the years, now resulting in various bottlings of Glen Grant vintages, some 50 years old and more. The Glen Grant is also readily available as a distillery bottling.

The Italian connection began in 1961 when Glen Grant manager at the time Douglas Mackessack met Armando Giovinetti, an Italian wine and spirits merchant. Both gentlemen made this single malt a very strong brand in Italy and at a certain moment more than half of Glen Grant's output was exported to Giovinetti's home country. The brand became so important in Italy that the venerable family-owned Campari company decided to buy the distillery in 2006 for the tidy sum of $1,550,000. Unfortunately the takeover coincided with a steep decline of Glen Grant sales. In the next few years the total sales of Scotch whisky decreased by a staggering 30% in Italy alone. Campari didn't give up or lose confidence in its Scottish subsidiary. Instead they invested heavily in refurbishing the visitor centre, updating the packaging design, creating new labelling and focusing on marketing. About 50% of the output is destined for blending, with a large proportion going into Chivas Regal. Not surprising since Chivas owner Pernod Ricard had Glen Grant before selling it to Campari.

When Becky suggested we take a holiday in Italy, a country that had no whisky distilleries at the time, arguing, 'If there are no distilleries, you won't be tempted to work,' she wasn't thinking about the above facts. After the usual friendly tug-of-war between your Whisky Couple – I always want to go north and Becky prefers the southern climates, being a true Southern belle after all – during which I voted for Sweden, which has distilleries I hadn't seen yet, and Becky stood firm for Italy, I finally gave in, thinking I might do a little field research in finding out if Glen Grant was still big there.

We packed our bags, got the car and drove from Zwolle to Altidona on the Adriatic coast – a mere 1,200 miles to cover. We took three days for the journey, choosing a scenic route and driving with top down through Germany, Liechtenstein and Austria, before crossing the mighty Dolomites. A fast run on the autostrada passing the boring but unavoidable Po delta took us to the Adriatic side of Italy where we followed the coast to Ancona. South of that city we took the Pedaso exit and followed a beautiful meandering road into the hills, passing the old village of Altidona and arriving at our destination – a charming villa in the hills of La Marche, where we would dogsit for Becky's high school friend Gina Steedley Wills for two weeks. She is married to Tim, a European and a whisky enthusiast, so the ladies have a lot in common.

On their balcony we enjoyed a view of the Adriatic Sea when looking left and the Sibylline Mountains when looking right. A perfect place to relax and unwind after some extremely busy years. A few days later the Wills left for England with their triplets, George, Hamish and Steedley, to visit family and we had the villa to ourselves, kept company by two wonderful Italian sheep dogs, Dixie and Delilah.

The first days we enjoyed being at the villa, cooking pasta at a leisurely pace, reading books, listening to music and just being content resting in such beautiful surroundings.

Then, according to me, it was time for some action. In this case, checking out some liquor stores, bars and restaurants to find out if the Italians still drank Glen Grant by the case. We always look at the shelves in bars, a mild form of professional deformation, so it came as no surprise to Becky when I pointed at a large bottle of Glen Grant 5-year-old when we were sitting in a nice little bar in a village not far from the villa, enjoying a morning coffee. 'See that?' I exclaimed, just a tiny bit too loud to not rouse her suspicion. 'What's with the enthusiasm?' she asked, raising her delicately formed left eyebrow. 'Ah, you know about Glen Grant,' I tried to escape. 'We're on vacation,' was the short reply. 'Have another cappuccino, dear,' I offered and ordered two more, before proceeding to tell my plans about field research. Becky sighed, patted me on the knee and grinned wickedly, 'Just drop me off at the beach, take care of your Italian job and pick me up later.'

Well, I did find Glen Grant everywhere. The Italians seem to drink it like lemonade and have a fondness for the 5-year-old and the un-aged version, which is probably even younger. I must say that I do enjoy it better at 12 years old, but the younger expressions are quite drinkable. They already have that sweet vanilla touch and a slightly nutty flavour that becomes more apparent in the older vintages. 90% of Glen Grant matures in ex-bourbon casks, which explains the floral and vanilla tones.

In Altidona's super market Glen Grant stood on the shelves next to Long John and... Glen Horney. I had to look twice but that was really what the label showed. Studying the back label I found out it was a Scotch blend, especially produced for the Italian market. That happens often. Supermarkets want their proprietary brands and often hire a Scottish whisky consultant to help them. These people usually come up with the name, too. The person taking care of this particular brand must have had a wicked sense of humour and the Italian importer may not have mastered the English language in the way he should. I grinned and took a photograph, which I put to good use some months later in a series of articles about whisky labels.

My research not only revealed lots of Glen Grant but also many other, sometimes hidden treasures, like a 1970s Macallan in a Loreto convenience store. One evening we headed to an ancient, hilltop fortified village – the area of La Marche is littered with them and they all have their own charm – where we ended up at the little market square. A podium was set up and we listened to an Italian Dixieland band playing old-style jazz. We ran into some friends of Gina and Tim's and I offered to get drinks from the tiny bar at the back of the square.

When I entered and looked at the shelves, I couldn't believe my eyes. Next to one another were some rare expressions of Scotland's finest: a 25-year-old Talisker, Johnnie Walker Blue Label King George V and a vintage Port Ellen from the long closed Islay distillery of the same name. That was something: nearly 1,200 miles from home and finding those gems in an 11th century village, safely tucked away in the Italian countryside. Treasures that one usually finds in specialist retail shops or high-end restaurants. When I came outside, the band started to play the 'Washington and Lee Swing' – the fight song from Becky and Gina's high school. It was one of those surreal moments in time. 'Whisky and Jazz. Indeed, it can be an Italian Job, too.', whispered the Famous Spouse in my ear.

Writing about Whisky

According to my friend and fellow whisky writer Charles MacLean in the past 20 years more books on whisky were published than in the previous 200 years. It's a fact, whisky is 'hot' so not only the liquor branch wants to profit from the boom, but the book trade as well. The number of books and booklets about whisky that appeared over the last couple of years offers something for every whisky-minded reader.

Having been a professional writer for more than 35 years myself, I can truly say that there is a lot of whisky in my books as well as in the author, albeit that I only started to seriously write about whisky around the turn of the millennium. Before that time I mainly considered it as entertainment, wrote various articles about the cratur, published a part work on whisky labels in Scotland in 1998, but it never crossed my mind to write intensively about my favourite drink, until my then-publisher suggested I should write a whole book about whisky and translate a couple of English whisky books into Dutch on the side. So, in 2003 my first complete whisky book was launched in Dutch and English. *The Road to Craigellachie* is something between a road-novel and a travelogue through Scotland and the world of whisky at the same time. Amazingly enough it is still in demand and we get emails from people around the world who took the book with them to Scotland, to check if what I'd written down was actually true. Since it is written in a narrative style, it seems a bit unusual that it's used as a travel guide, although I put three routes in the back of the book with recommendations on where to go and which roads to take. Dominic Roskrow, at the time editor-in-chief, reviewed it for *Whisky Magazine* as follows: 'It is an oddball of a book, but I really liked it!'

When the book sold out, I published an updated edition in 2011, titled *The Road to Craigellachie Revisited*. During the annual Spirit of Speyside Festival we climbed Ben Rinnes with a group of whisky enthusiasts. On the top I handed the first copy to my fellow scribe and whisky friend Dave Broom. In 2016 we launched a special limited Quaich Edition of *The Road*, to celebrate the resurrection of the Craigellachie Hotel and the refurbishing of its famed Quaich Bar.

As of today I have written and/or translated over 25 whisky books and approximately 60 books in total, about various topics, ranging from the salvage of a Russian nuclear submarine to a 450-page novel following a man's many changes of address while constantly getting into humorous situations. If you enjoy John Irving, you might enjoy The House, too. About 10 years ago I stopped counting how many articles I have written.

People often ask me where I get my inspiration. Some of it just 'pops up' from the unconscious, another part is triggered by things I read in the newspaper, or stories told to me by others. A walk in the woods or on the beach is a very fine preparation before I go back to my writing desk.

Recently Becky re-catalogued our collection of drinks books and counted a staggering 500-something volumes, of which more than 450 treat the subject whisky. We use our drinks library as a source of inspiration as well. In writing a column or article we often choose a book on a certain topic and leaf through it. In most cases we find what we are – unconsciously – looking for. Call it serendipity if you want. I do the first draft, then Becky edits and comes with suggestions to improve the text. A second version is made and Becky gives a final verdict before we send it off to the magazine or newspaper that requested a piece. So, although I write in the first person, a lot of my English pieces are actually co-written by the other half of The Whisky Couple.

Well, here are some nice tips about fine whisky books. Some old, some new.

The 'grandfather' of contemporary whisky writers is Alfred Barnard. In the 1880's he undertook a two-year-journey to write his 457-page tome *The Whisky Distilleries of the United Kingdom*. This title is extremely rare to acquire and first editions sell between £1,000 and £1,500, depending on the condition of the book. Luckily a couple of German whisky aficionados brought this book back to life in a facsimile publication in 2001 at an affordable price. The American gentleman Aaron Barker, whose initials are coincidentally the same as Barnard's, devoted a whole facebook page to his literary whisky hero and also brought this seminal book to life in a facsimile edition. Since Barnard left the building more than 75 years ago, there are no longer royalties involved.

Another whisky book lover and expert on the drink is Ian Buxton. Together with Scottish publisher and whisky writer Neil Wilson he created Classicexpressions.co.uk and re-published a series of delightful pearls of the past, among which *Reminiscences of a Gauger* (1873) by Joseph Pacy. A gauger is a person who tries to catch illicit distillers. They are not well liked in the Scottish Highlands. A second example from the hands of Buxton and Wilson is *Smuggling in the Highlands* (1914) from Ian MacDonald. For many centuries smuggling was considered an honorable profession in the Highlands and Islands of Scotland. The 1824 Act passed by the British Government ended it all. Glenlivet took a license as one of the first and was hated for that by its direct neighbours, but 10-12 years later the illicit still was reduced to a rare phenomenon. Nowadays there is a tour around The Glenlivet that includes a trek along the old smuggling routes in the valley and surrounding hills.

My dear late friend and mentor Michael Jackson left a

beautiful legacy of books and I can especially recommend *The Malt Whisky Companion*, 5th edition and *WHISKY - The Definitive World Guide*. The former title is a tasting guide with descriptions of more than 1,000 single malts. The latter is an encyclopaedic approach to the subject and contains beautiful pictures of distilleries around the world.

One of my favourite whisky books was written by Scotsman Dr. David Wishart and first published in 2004. It is called *Whisky Classified*. Wishart developed a standard taste profile, consisting of 12 key components. Using his profile he tested over 100 single malt whiskies and scored them using an intensity scale from zero to four. Then he divided them into several taste groups, by means of cluster analysis, a method often applied in biology. The taste profile gives a good indication in which cluster a specific whisky belongs. Wishart describes 10 clusters, named A to J, which are a handy tool to compare one whisky with another. On the author's website one can download software called 'Whisky Analyst'. This program lets the user score every whisky or whiskey he wants to try. Wishart's book is an international success and he can boast Finnish, Swedish, Danish, Dutch, Italian and Chinese editions. No need to say who got to translate the Dutch edition.

For my book, *A Taste of Whisky*, published in 2007, I compared Jackson's approach with Wishart's method. The first one is based on personal experience, the second one on a scientific exercise and it is interesting to read both experts' conclusions. Michael Jackson always emphasised the fact that his approach was very subjective. David Wishart's method seems more objective, although the intensity score is arbitrary. In the end, the only taste that really matters is yours.

To give you an idea of whisky and distilling literature through the ages, I will end this chapter with a historical list of about 50 whisky publications, in chronological order. Many of these authors have written more than one book; generally I included their first significant contribution. Bear in mind Charlie's remark about the explosion of whisky books in the past two decades.

1512 Hieronymus Braunschweig – *The Virtuous Book of Distillation*

1718 author unknown – *The Practical Distiller*

1873 Joseph Pacy – *Reminiscences of a Gauger*

1887 Alfred Barnard – *The Whisky Distilleries of the United Kingdom*

1913 J.A. Nettleton – *The Manufacture of Whisky and Plain Spirit*

1914 Ian Macdonald – *Smuggling in the Highlands*

1920 George Saintsbury – *Notes on a Cellar-Book*

1930 Aeneas Macdonald – *Whisky*

1935 Neil Gunn – *Whisky and Scotland*

1951 Sir Robert Bruce Lockhart - *Scotch*

1965 Frank Kane – *Anatomy of the Whisky Business*

1968 Emmanuel Greenberg – *Whisky in the Kitchen*

1969 David Dachies – *Scotch Whisky*

1970 James Ross – *Whisky*

1971 R.J.S. McDowall – *The Whiskies of Scotland*

1978 Fred Steneker – *Whisky*

1981 Michael Moss & John R. Hume – *The Making of Scotch Whisky*

1985 Wallace Milroy – *Malt Whisky Almanac* [1]

1985 Neil Wilson – *Scotch & Water*

1987 Michael Jackson - *The World Guide to Whisky* [2]

1991 David Milsted – *Bluff Your Way in Whisky*

1991 first volume of *Malt Advocate* magazine (published as Whisky Advocate since 2011)

1992 Tom Morton – *A Journey beyond the Whisky Trails*

1992 Charles MacLean – *Scotch Whisky*
1993 Gavin D. Smith – *Whisky – A Book of Words*
1993 Brian Townsend – *Scotch Missed*
1995 John Lamond and Robin Tucek – *The Malt Whisky File*
1995 Gary Regan et al – *The Book of Bourbon*
1997 Helen Arthur – *Single Malt Whisky Companion*
1997 Jim Murray – *The Complete Guide to Whisky* [3]
1998 Dave Broom – *A Connoisseurs Guide*
1998 Hans Offringa – *The Craigellachie Collection of Whisky Labels*
1998 first volume of *Whisky Magazine*
1999 Martine Nouet – *Les Routes du Malt*
2000 Phillip Hills – *Appreciating Whisky*
2002 Ian Buxton - *Whisky, History, Hints & Tips - A Handy Guide*
2002 Robin Laing – *The Whisky Muse*
2002 Peter Mulryan – *The Whiskeys of Ireland*
2002 David Wishart – *Whisky Classified*
2003 first volume of *Whisky Etc.* magazine
2004 Bob Minnekeer – *Whisky a la carte*
2005 Ingvar Ronde – *Malt Whisky Yearbook*
2006 first volume of *Whisky Passion*
2008 Sheila McConachie and Graham Harvey – *The Whisky Kitchen*
2009 Dominic Roskrow – *From Confused to Connoisseur*
2010 Igor Maltsev – *Whisky*
2011 Heidi Donelon – *Ultimate Guide to Irish Whiskey*
2012 Davin de Kergommaux – *Canadian Whisky, the Portable Expert*
2013 Fred Minnick – *Whiskey Women*
2013 Neil Ridley and Gavin D. Smith – *Let Me Tell You about Whisky*
2014 Lew Bryson – *Tasting Whisky*
2014 Heather Greene – *Whisk(e)y Distilled*

2014 Inge Russell and Graham Stewart – *Whisky - Technology, Production and Marketing*

2014 Ralph Warth – *Liquid Gold – Investing Successfully in Whisky*

2015 Fionnan O'Connor – *A Glass Apart - Irish Single Pot Still Whiskey*

---

[1] Wallace asked Michael Jackson to be a co-author, but the latter didn't have time; he first had to finish his seminal work on beer.

[2] Two years later, in 1989, Michael's much lauded *Malt Whisky Companion* was published for the first time. Eventually he completed five editions.

[3] The first *Whisky Bible* appeared in 2003.

How Independent Is Independent?

That question is frequently asked of the Whisky Couple during whisky festivals as well as on internet whisky forums. The latest reason for such a question was the presentation of a new edition of our *Whisky Almanak* in The Netherlands. In one of the forums concerned, comments were made about the almanak's earlier editions and how the whiskies and whiskeys therein were chosen.

Are we independent in the compiling of whisky books such as the *Almanak*? Yes, surely. Are we depending on others? That as well, albeit in a limited way. Our old and trusted friend Mr Ad de Koning, founder and one time managing director of the Scotch Single Malt Whiskey Society – formerly the society of whisk(e)y importers in The Netherlands – stands by virtue of his profession in the whisky field, but is dependent on that which is furnished by the importers. Nowadays many premium whiskies are on allotment per country or per retail outlet. It means you can only get your hand – and mouth – around some expressions when you travel a lot internationally and have a wallet to match. Since our *Almanak* is only intended for the Dutch and Flemish markets, we refrain from putting in whiskies or whiskeys that are hardly or not at all available in The Netherlands or Belgium. A comparison with independent bottlers comes to mind. They decide when it's time to bottle a whisky, but depend on the distilleries that might or might not want to sell them specific casks. In the end the latter is the factor that determines whether they offer a whisky.

A significant portion of our books and articles deals with whiskey and whisky. We decide what we write, whether it is about a specific whisky, a general subject or a related issue. Research about the subject is, with the writing of books

as well as articles, a matter of substance. Acquiring cooperation of authorities that are related to the subject area goes without saying and adds important value to a book. For example, I could never have written the historical book *Raising the Kursk* without the cooperation of experts from Mammoet, Smit International, the Russian Navy and the Russian Ministry of Defence, as well as some Scottish divers.

The condition for my accepting that assignment was to get 'carte blanche' when describing the history of the salvage of the *Kursk*. I got a free hand indeed and went to Russia to interview relatives of the departed seamen, technical engineers, the designer of the *Kursk*, Mr Igor Baranov and Mr Igor Spassky, right hand of President Putin and CEO of Rubin, the design company of the Russian Navy. They allowed me to dig up all the material I needed and there was no censorship whatsoever. I could bring home all video and photo material unscreened by the authorities.

At the airport in St Petersburg however, a small incident happened before departure. My cameraman hadn't cleared his equipment when we'd flown into Russia. The customs officer claimed it with the remark: 'Since this camera is not officially in our country, it cannot leave Russia', obviously wanting to appropriate the equipment himself. My man panicked and motioned me to come back, but I was holding two plastic bags with 24 videotapes and there was no going back for me! Luckily the press official of Mammoet Company, who had accompanied us on the trip, knew how to deal with it. She called CEO Frans van Seumeren who immediately got in touch with Rubin. It took five minutes for the customs man to apologise and let the cameraman pass, with his equipment. Well, after having raised the *Kursk* and having brought home the bodies of the 118 sailors who perished in the accident, the Van Seumerens are heroes in Russia, and that has its advantages.

The cooperation of an industry is not an (in)dependency matter. It is something completely different: a *conditio sine qua non*. That applies to the *Kursk*, but also to the *Whisky Almanak* or other (whiskey) publications of ours.

It might occur from time to time that we write for a specific spirits company. That can be a book, a website or a one-off printed publication. The content of the publication is determined in dialogue with the client. In this, the cooperation of the constituent is, regarding the research, very important. For instance we were able to write the small book *Classic Malts Selection*, which exclusively deals with 27 Scotch single malt distilleries of Diageo, because Diageo offered us the possibility of travelling to their international headquarters in London in order to search their digital archives and make selections of photos. In our field that's just called cooperation, not dependency.

The Legend of Laphroaig, which we wrote with the extensive assistance of fellow Dutchman Marcel van Gils, the world's largest Laphroaig collector, could only become a 206-page tome because the distillery, as well as American owner Beam Global, gave us permission to access their historical files at the library of Glasgow University and on the Isle of Islay. For us it meant not only days and days of going through old documents and photographs, coming from a period between 1820 and 2007, but also interviewing people currently working at Laphroaig, taking many pictures, strolling on the distillery grounds around midnight, sharing an anecdote with the stillman on duty. It's part of our – delightful – job, but it doesn't mean that we willingly accept everything that is told to us. We check, re-check, double-check, triple-check before it goes to print. *The Legend of Laphroaig* is a true account of the history of the eponymous distillery, with all its ups and downs. We can only be thankful for so much cooperation and involvement, not interference! More can be read about this in the chapter 'The Making of *The Legend of Laphroaig*.'

About scoring whiskies and giving awards, many insinuations have been whispered, written and spoken out loud. For instance that high scores mean improper involvement of the respective author(s) with certain whisk(e)y producers. Bollocks! We cannot afford to be biased, since we work for the industry at large.

By the way, there are pros and cons for the scoring method. We don't use a scoring system ourselves. In the *Whiskey Almanak* we try to give an objective, detailed description, which in only a small degree gives a direction to the consumer concerning type and taste of the contents of the bottle. Taste after all is and will always be a personal thing. We do mark whiskeys with a star when we think the price/quality ratio is optimal. Apart from that it is true that taste changes per season, and also over a longer period of time. Research has proven that the taste buds of a human being change approximately every ten years. That appears to be the same for fashion, living arts and literature. This doesn't have to mean that you don't appreciate the things from the past, but other dimensions are added. Some others disappear. A long-forgotten single malt can become a favourite again when re-acquainted and a current fave might be a bit disappointing after a while.

The beauty of the (whiskey) world is, seen through our eyes, a multi-dimensional one. And whether a writer likes a whiskey or not is not important. I write fiction and nonfiction. In a certain way that keeps me in balance as a writer.

A balance between fantasy and reality, supported by regularly consuming a glass of whisky. Preferably different ones. Only for balance. And independence, as you will understand.

Whisky Galore

On 4 February 1941, 4 am, the *S.S. Politician* ran aground in the Sound of Eriskay, a narrow sea street between the islands Eriskay and South Uist, part of the outer Hebrides, Scotland. A day earlier the merchant ship had left Mersey harbour, England, with orders to meet a convoy north of Scotland and join them in crossing the Atlantic with final destination Jamaica. Research 20 years later, most notably by renowned English journalist Arthur Swinson, revealed that magnetic rocks in the Hebrides might have corrupted the compass on board and were the main reason that the Polly, as the ship was affectionately nicknamed, was thrown off course more than 20 degrees and subsequently crashed into a huge rock.

The event spawned a novel 15 years before Swinson's findings. Scottish author Sir Compton Mackenzie used to live on the isle of Barra near the place of the accident and was inspired to write about it. He published *Whisky Galore* as 'a modern fairy tale' in 1947. The book was a great success and turned into a movie in 1949. In the USA the book and film were called Tight Little Island because a ban existed at the time preventing the use of an alcoholic drink's name in the title.

The book still sells. That is no surprise, since the story holds many elements that make for good reading. Here are some plain facts. The cargo of the Polly consisted of cars, bicycles, clothes and ... 22,000 cases of Scotch whisky! That means approximately 240,000 bottles of our favourite tipple. The entire crew was saved and taken to the mainland within a couple of days, but word had gone to the islanders that there was an interesting cargo aboard. For centuries the Hebrideans considered a shipwreck and its contents 'theirs,' so many a little boat set out to the Polly at night to 'rescue' its precious cargo, as the islanders euphemistically called the looting party. It didn't take long before the Customs and Excise department of the United Kingdom took action. The one officer in the region, a Mr McColl, was relentless in pursuing the 'thieves' and tried to intercept the little vessels where and when he could. Since they came from all the surrounding islands (even as far as Mull), McColl had a mission impossible at hand. For months to come, the little islands near the place where the Polly prematurely ended its journey were drowned in whisky. The inhabitants were reportedly drunk most of the time and more than a few casualties were the consequence of the 24 hours a day inebriety. Most islanders developed cunning tricks to mislead the Customs officers when they visited their crofts. Bottles were hung in chimneys, buried in the peat bogs up the hills and some inventive and unscrupulous ones even hid their stash in coffins, temporarily moving the corpses under their beds.

To the astonishment of the islanders, the insurance company and owners were not interested in salvaging the whisky, since it might have been polluted with seawater. At least that was what those gentlemen far, far away in London thought. Little did they know.

In the meantime McColl and his superior, Excise men to the core, were very worried about whisky being consumed without tax being paid by the 'new owners' and they managed to get about 50 islanders sentenced for theft. Although they were all caught red-handed, records of the court show a strange way of dealing with the sentences. The majority of the 'crooks' were dismissed on the pretext that there was not enough evidence. However, some of the men, who were in the same boats when they were caught, were either fined or sent to prison for a month or two. It seems pride and prejudice co-existed in that court.

Of course the Whisky Galore party could not continue

and a decision was made to end it with a blast. An order was given to put dynamite in the wreck and blow the remaining cases of whisky to pieces. That was like adding insult to injury to many an islander and one of them was reputed to have commented at the time 'Dynamiting whisky! You wouldn't think there'd be men in the world so crazy as *that*!'

Well, anyway, that was what happened. Many a Highland Glen, Stag's Head, Haig and Dimple bottle were blown to pieces eight months after the accident. As a rough estimate, the islanders 'rescued' about one third of the cargo, around 80,000 bottles! Many years later, bottles of the '*Polly* whisky' were still in the peat bogs, forgotten or unable to be found back by their new owners..

On these facts Sir Compton Mackenzie based his highly entertaining novel *Whisky Galore*. Of course he changed names of people and islands involved and poured a romantic sauce over the entire story. I have different editions in my library, among which a Canongate hardcover edition from 1999. Inside the book a miniature bottle of Dewar's Scotch is hidden. It was a creative concept from my Scottish colleague Ian Buxton, who regularly does marketing stuff for Dewar's. He also wrote a beautiful book about the history of that brand, titled *The Enduring Legacy of Dewar's*. Canongate's *Whisky Galore* edition ran aground quickly, just like the *Polly*. Nobody at the marketing bureau, nor the author, nor the publisher had realised that book stores are not allowed to sell liquor, hence the book was never seen in stores apart from the shop at Aberfeldy Distillery, the spiritual home of Dewar's.

Whisky Galore did however inspire the English journalist Arthur Swinson to investigate what was truth and what was fiction in this particular case. In 1963 he published his own book about it, after having done thorough research in situ and interviewing many people directly involved, such as islanders, crew and McColl's superior, Mr Gledhill, who was still alive at the time (McColl had died some years earlier). Swinson's book was titled *Scotch on the Rocks, The True Story Behind Whisky Galore.* It gave Sir Compton Mackenzie 'great pleasure to write the foreword to Mr Arthur Swinson's dogged pursuit of the facts about the *S.S. Politician* and in doing so to be able to testify to the accuracy with which he has told what everybody will surely find an absorbing tale.' Swinson sadly died in 1970 of a sudden heart attack, aged only 54. *Scotch on the Rocks* went into obscurity.

Then, in 1990, something truly strange happened. Mainstream Publishing published a book titled *Polly, The True Story Behind Whisky Galore*, written by, again, a journalist. This time it was a certain Robert Hutchinson. Remarkable, since not only did he practically steal the title of Swinson's book, but the publication had a very strong smell of plagiarism, although new pieces of information were added. The author even goes so far as to state in writing that *Whisky Galore* should have been titled *Scotch on the Rocks.* That unmitigated audacity truly shocked me.

Hutchinson's copy (pun intended) is still available. Luckily Swinson's daughter Antonia decided a few years ago to revive her father's legacy and gave Luath Press Ltd, Edinburgh, permission to re-publish his work. A respected journalist in her own right, Mrs Swinson added a special introduction to the 2005 edition, with a pen dipped in vitriol. She 'literally' kills off Sir Compton Mackenzie. According to her he did not do the islanders a favour with his romanticised story. There was only one person who had told the truth – her father Arthur Swinson. As she agitatedly states, his book 'has never been surpassed', although she does not mention Hutchinson by name. Well, no offense, but the British are champions of implied messages, aren't they?

Being a writer of fiction *and* non-fiction, I can cordially recommend all three books and suggest you read them in chronological order. Mackenzie knows how to bind the reader with his fantasy, Swinson has a very enjoyable style of presenting facts and Hutchinson did dig up some new facts.

Not all mysteries surrounding the *Polly* have been revealed over time. For instance what happened to the fortune in 10-shilling Jamaican bank notes, stashed away between clothes, bales of cotton and whisky cases? One story is that the money was meant for the Royal Family, in case Adolf Hitler conquered Great Britain and they were forced to go into exile. This remains speculative, but for many years these bank notes showed up in Britain, where people asked their bank to exchange them for British pounds.

Of course it is no way to end this remarkable story by suggesting that the British royalty would ever consider the possibility of the British army losing a war. Therefore I will end this chapter with an appropriate original Gaelic ballad by Roddy Campbell, translated by Hebridean Norman MacMillan and anglicised by Arthur Swinson.

The Song of the Politician

Don't ask me why I am feeling sad,
My thoughts are melancholy.
The truth is that I've had a dram
Of whisky from the *Polly*.
For that's the ship that came ashore,
And you never saw her like before –
She'd whisky in the hold galore
And it's led me into folly!

When they brought the news that she was there
I took my boat to board her;
Found silk and cotton, sherry, stout,
And fine goods ranged in order.
But down there in the flooded end
Was every kind of brand or blend
That God or a kindly fate could send –
And me the first marauder!

'Twas clear to me and clear to all
That ship was wrecked for ever;
And if we left the whisky there
It would be tasted never.
But soon the Customs came around
And though I'd hit it underground
My stock of good 'Spey Royal' they found –
And I thought I'd been so clever!

So to Lochmaddy Court I went,
Bewildered and outwitted.
The Fiscal stood and read the charge
But I would not admit it.
The policemen stood around there tense
While the Customs gave their evidence –
But the Sheriff said it didn't make sense
And so I was acquitted!

So here's a health to the Captain bold
Of the good ship Politician!
And here's to the rock she struck that night,
A-saling on her mission!

What's left of her can still be found
Off Calvay Isle in Eriskay Sound;
Of all great ships she is renowned –
The *Polly*!
The *Polly*!
We shall not see her like again
Though we live from now to a hundred and ten,
The good ship *Politician*!

Port William
A 714 (A 7085)

Whithorn
A 714 (A 746) →

◀ Martyrs'
Stake

P

Bladnoch
Visitor Centr

◀ Wigtown Bay
Visitor Centre
80 yds

ILLKOMMEN
AILTE
ENVENUE

Welcome to
SCOTLAND'S
NATIONAL
BOOK TOWN

BENV
W
BIEN

A Town Full of Books – and Whisky

From The Netherlands it is relatively easy to travel to Scotland. Aberdeen, Glasgow and Edinburgh are within 1 hour and 15 minutes by plane from Amsterdam-Schiphol airport. Even Inverness can be reached in a couple of hours, albeit that one often has to endure a stopover at the dreaded Luton Terminal north of London. Another means of transport is the DFDS ferry. It leaves IJmuiden – 15 miles from Amsterdam – every afternoon around 5 pm and arrives in Newcastle, England the next morning 9-9:30 am (depending on weather) local time. It is a very comfortable trip and we prefer it to flying. Once you have boarded with your car, you can have a wee dram in the bar, followed by a tasty two or three course dinner, a night cap in the bar with musical entertainment and then 7-8 hours of sleep in your cabin. The following morning, during breakfast, the ferry turns into the mouth of the River Tyne, mooring 30 minutes later at the northern quay.

In 2009 we were invited to the Wigtown Book Festival in Dumfries-and-Galloway, a largely overlooked part of Scotland. This is a shame since it is a gorgeous area, with mountains, sea, forests and, most important of all, a very nice, old and authentic distillery: Bladnoch.

Wigtown is only a three-hour drive from Newcastle, straight to the west. Since we had to carry quite a few books we decided to take the ferry. The weather was good to us and after a quiet journey we drove via Hadrian's Wall – built by the late Roman Emperor to keep the wild Scots out of England, although many a Scot will tell you that it was to keep the English in – to Dumfries, the capital of this most south west region of Scotland. From there it is a mere 50 miles south to Wigtown.

The Wigtown Book Festival was celebrating its 11th edition and has become a lifeline for the region. Only a decade ago the small town with the surprisingly large County Buildings looked rather dilapidated. But then, by miracle, Wigtown was named 'the book capital of Scotland' and book stores, second hand and new, mushroomed in the surrounding streets. Nowadays it is a gold mine for first editions of long forgotten authors or celebrated ones. The Book Festival has grown year by year, attracting famous Scottish authors like the late Iain Banks (*The Wasp Factory*, *The Crow Road*), better known in the USA as Iain M. Banks, the Sci-Fi author.

The year 2009 was the great Homecoming Year for the Scots and festival director Adrian Turpin decided early that year to organise a little festival-within-a-festival, calling it 'Whisky & Words.' We were honoured by his invitation to speak about several of our books, most notably *Whisky & Jazz* and *The Legend of Laphroaig*. Apart from that it meant a reunion with fellow scribes Charles MacLean and Dave Broom, the two most famous Scottish whisky writers to date, carrying with them the legacy of our dear mutual friend and colleague, the late and great Michael Jackson (1941-2007).

The beauty of it all was that the whisky venues were held inside Bladnoch Distillery, with the cooperation of then-owner Raymond Armstrong and his wife Florence. Thanks to this friendly and determined Irish couple, Bladnoch, the southernmost distillery in Scotland, is still alive today. In 1993 then-owner United Distillers (now part of Diageo) decided to concentrate its Lowland malt activities at Glenkinchie distillery, in the east, 20 miles from Edinburgh. Rosebank, near Falkirk, and Bladnoch were mothballed. The former was eventually sold, partly demolished and all distilling equipment taken out, but Bladnoch was spared that humiliation. In 1994 Raymond – who owns a construction company in Northern Ireland - passed the pretty little eponymous village and saw the distillery manager's house for sale. He instantly liked it and made an offer. As an aside he inquired if the distillery and warehouses were for sale too and they were. Raymond decided to buy the entire lot, except for the maturing whisky. His original plan was to convert the buildings into holiday cottages, but instead he fell in love with the silent distillery and wanted to revive it again.

Alas, there was a clause in the contract with the former owner that there could be no such thing as distilling Bladnoch whisky in this place ever again. With Irish stubbornness and determination Mr Armstrong went on a crusade. It took him six years to convince behemoth Diageo to give him permission, during which time he simply turned down one offer after another because parts of the agreement were not to his liking. He knew where he was going and on what terms he wanted to achieve his goal. In December 2000 the proverbial Irish David had slain Multinational Goliath and the stills ran again, under the watchful eye of former distiller John. Slowly the Armstrongs started to renovate the distillery, leaving the old atmosphere intact.

To render some cash Raymond bought old casks of maturing Bladnoch and other single malts, bottling them and selling them in the nice visitor centre, where he also opened a coffee shop. Furthermore Raymond started to let out warehouse space to other distillers for their ever-increasing stocks. All in all he got a good thing going, meanwhile commuting between his house in North Ireland, south of Belfast and the village of Bladnoch. That seems far but the ferry to Belfast leaves from Stranraer, a mere 26 miles from Bladnoch. It is possible to leave in the morning, visit Bushmills Distillery in Antrim County, have a look at the Giant's Causeway and be back in Scotland the same evening.

When Becky and I arrived at the festival we had to report to the County Buildings in Wigtown first, to collect our

BLADNOCH
DISTILLERY
Spirit of the Lowlands

CENTRE   SHOP   TOURS

PRIVATE PROPERTY

'goody bag,' as Adrian Turpin had said, and to receive directions to the cottage where we were to stay for five days. Wigtown is two miles from Bladnoch and Orchard Cottage three miles again from the distillery. But no driving under the influence ! The festival organisation had arranged for a taxi wherever we wanted to go during the festivities. We dearly needed that because the evening of our arrival we were to attend a Burns Supper in the main hall.

It was a remarkable one, and the first ever we attended where the haggis went missing. After 10 minutes of desperate bagpipe playing with no haggis appearing, the Robert Burns impersonator went to check in the kitchen himself and reappeared in the hall five minutes later ... with a steamin' and gleamin' haggis, addressing the little creature in pure Gaelic. He was so drunk that he didn't notice one of his sideburns had disappeared; things with him would go from bad to worse.

We were seated at the writers' table with Raymond and Florence Armstrong amidst us all. Needless to say the evening was marinated in Bladnoch whisky of various vintages, among which an excellent 16-year-old. Various speakers, one more under the influence than the other, put up a formal speech. So did Mr 'Burns'. He suddenly found it necessary to verbally attack a lady who had just delivered her own version of Tam 'o' Shanter. So, the next speaker did the same to 'Burns' who then got a bit savage and was decidedly taken out of the room by a couple of sturdy Lowlanders. We did not see him that evening anymore. Much later a friendly cab driver delivered a very happy Whisky Couple safe and sound at Orchard Cottage.

The following days were spent mostly in the distillery where we lectured about whisky and presented and signed our books, thanks to Beverley Chadband of GC Books, who arranged that wherever at the festival we showed up, our books were on display. One afternoon we were part of a true whisky writers' panel, led by Ian Buxton, publisher of Classic Expressions, a company he runs with the well-known Scottish whisky book publisher and writer Neil Wilson. Buxton earned his spurs with Glenmorangie and designed the famous Dewar's World of Whisky in Aberfeldy. He showed himself an eloquent and very funny speaker, teasing his colleagues and challenging audience and scribes to participate in hearty banter. Such a get together is rare for this small band of international whisky writers. Usually we communicate via email or mobile phone, one being in South Africa, another in India, number three in Japan and number four in the USA. We hardly see each other at the same time, and surely not four days on a stretch, so we decided to end the day with a joint dinner in a seafood restaurant outside Wigtown, suggested by Neil Wilson.

The final event of the Whisky & Words part of the Wigtown Book Festival was the presentation of the first Bladnoch single malt whisky distilled under the ownership of Raymond Armstrong and his right-hand men John and Hugh: an 8-year-old, distilled in December 2000 and bottled on 3 October 2009, in a limited edition of 250 only, of which one was given to us by Florence Armstrong. I had it signed by Raymond and John immediately. The label shows a stack of books.

The next day our fellow writers left and we had a few extra days to spend before returning to catch the ferry at Newcastle. When we came to say goodbye to Raymond and Florence, they invited us for a wee walk in the Galloway Hills. Again the weather was our friend and the four of us spent the entire afternoon outside, fatiguing their sheepdog, Whisky. The Irish couple really had rooted themselves in this underestimated part of Scotland and they proudly showed us around Wigtown later that day – Raymond telling anecdote after engaging anecdote. He is a true storyteller, as most Irish are. Here's a little ditty he shared that afternoon: 'One time, a long time before he became owner of Bladnoch there was a distillery manager who happened to be a bit too fond of his own product. He often drove his car after whisky fuelled events and parties in and around Bladnoch Village. These were the 1970s and legend has it that the police would regularly look the other way in certain circumstances. One evening however, said distillery manager had drunk such a staggering amount, that another guest decided to call the police before he had a chance to start his car. They promised to come as quickly as possible and soon appeared with two cars.' I interrupted Raymond, asking: 'This is a sparsely populated area of the country, isn't one car enough?' Raymond smiled and answered: 'No, you misunderstand. It was one car to drive in front of him and one to follow him on his way home!' Well, those were the days, but I would not recommend anyone follow that example.

The next day we took a round trip around the entire peninsula and made various stops underway. At the Mull of Galloway we climbed the lighthouse and could see the Five Kingdoms at the same time: England, Wales, Scotland, Ireland and the Kingdom of Heaven. Again the weather was gorgeous. That night we slept in a B&B in the artist's village of Kirkcudbright, much to the delight of Becky, since her favourite author Dorothy Sayers sends Lord Peter Wimsey to that picturesque little town in her novel *The Five Red Herrings*.

If you plan a trip to Scotland and you haven't made up your mind where to go yet, you should try Dumfries and Galloway. Alas, you won't find Raymond and Fiona Armstrong at the distillery anymore. Bladnoch was sold to an Australian company in 2015, after having been out of production for a couple of years.

A Dram at Fingal's Cave

The Isle of Mull, one of the inner Hebrides off the west coast of the Scottish mainland, harbours one small distillery that produces two different single malts: the unpeated Tobermory and the peated Ledaig. Tobermory started its life around 1798 as a brewery but soon changed to distilling whisky. It ran until 1837 after which a silent period followed until 1878, when the distillery was reopened. Tobermory changed hands a few times and was closed again in 1930, serving as a canteen and power station for the next 42 years.

In 1972 the buildings were refurbished by then-owner Spanish sherry producer Domecq, and whisky distilling started again, albeit under a new name: Ledaig Distillery. It wouldn't last long. After three years the company went bankrupt and closed again, this time for four years. In 1979 a real estate business acquired the distillery, rebaptised it into ... Tobermory and started up the stills again. Poor Tobermory. This time it closed after three years of uninterrupted production and in 1982 parts of the buildings were converted into apartments. A few warehouses were rented out to a dairy company that used the buildings for storing goods. The still house however stayed intact and remarkably, in 1989, distilling was resumed for the umptiest time.

In 1993 distillery and stocks were acquired by Burn Stewart Distillers and since then a steady stream of new make has flowed from the stills on this beautiful island. A major change was one of ownership (again) in 2002 when Burn Stewart was bought by CL Financial, a venture capitalist based in Trinidad. Getting Tobermory and Ledaig back on the market isn't easy, since there have been such serious gaps in production since Tobermory's inception. In 2013 Tobermory changed hands again when the South African company Distell Group Limited purchased the Burn Stewart Group.

Some years before I met Becky, I visited Tobermory. I enjoyed the old, laid back place and its picturesque little harbour, which reminded me of Portree harbour on the Isle of Skye, to the north of Mull, and home to that great peppery whisky Talisker. The distillery manager of Tobermory advised me to take a couple of days to explore the island and make a trip to nearby Iona and Staffa. I had heard of the former, an early Celtic-Christian place of worship and currently a place of pilgrimage. The latter literally sounded a 'bell' in the back of my head. I am very fond of Felix Mendelssohn's *Hebridean Overture*, which is said to have been inspired by his visit to Fingal's Cave on Staffa Island. I checked my diary and found some spare time. Hence, I set out on a little Christian and musical pilgrimage of my own.

Iona is quiet and beautiful, a serene place, ideal for contemplation. Although many tourists visit the place – it is only a five-minute crossing from the southwest tip of the Isle of Mull – this doesn't damage its serenity. I might dedicate a whole story to Iona in times to come.

When the weather permits, and that is not too often, one can take a small ferry to Staffa to admire Fingal's Cave. I was lucky that particular day and boarded, with about 20 other passengers, a boat that resisted the waves and delivered us safe and sound on the causeway of Staffa a mere hour later. I walked down the causeway, turned at the end and gazed in awe at the huge basalt formations that form the entrance of a huge cave. The tide was low, so I explored part of the inner cave that resembles a cathedral hewn out of basalt pillars. I can truly say it is one of the most amazing places I have ever seen during my many travels on the globe. In my mind I heard the first notes of Mendelssohn's famous composition, sat down on one of the lower pillars that form a natural seat and imbibed the atmosphere, unaware of other people sur-rounding me.

Although Staffa had been inhabited for several ages, it was the English scientist Joseph Banks who first described the island and its phenomenal structures after his initial visit in August 1772. Banks became very famous and was elected President of the Royal Society a mere six years later. For more than 40 years he held this post, until his death in 1820.

Staffa has had many owners and was part of the Ulva Estate long before written records were kept. In 1785 Colin MacDonald acquired the now uninhabited Staffa. Colin's son Ranald inherited the island and entertained famous Scottish writer Sir Walter Scott on the island several times. It led to Scott writing the following words about this amazing place ' ... one of the most extraordinary places I ever beheld. It exceeded, in my mind, every description I had heard of it ... composed entirely of basaltic pillars as high as the roof of a cathedral, and running deep into the rock, eternally swept by a deep and swelling sea, and paved, as it were, with ruddy marble, baffles all description.' Various poets and writers would follow in his footsteps among whom John Keats, Jules Verne, Robert Louis Stevenson and yours humbly.

Around 1978 Staffa was purchased by an American gen-tleman, Mr Jock Elliot Jr, at the time chairman of advertising company Ogilvy & Mather. When his wife Elly turned sixty in 1986, he decided to honour that occasion by donating Staffa to The National Trust of Scotland, which institution does its utmost to preserve this unique piece of the earth. That is a good thing because some of the former owners in-between the MacDonalds and Elliotts made serious plans to build a hotel and a small airstrip on the 80 acres small island. It would not only have destroyed one of the most beautiful places I have seen, but also an abundance of wildlife, among which the comical puffins that nest in numerous pairs on Staffa before returning to the Atlantic.

The guide from the boat awoke me from my contemplation saying, 'Sir, it's time to go for the boat. The tide is coming in and you won't survive in the cave if you stay here.' I sighed deeply, felt in my back pocket, drew out a small hip flask and offered it to the guide: 'It's from over yonder?' he smiled and pointed to the Isle of Mull. 'Yes, indeed,' I beamed and took a swig of Tobermory, looking one more time over my shoulder as we walked back to the little ferry, not knowing that I would return to this place in 2015, this time *with* Becky.

Speyburn and the Salmon

Angling is a sport in which I am not very experienced. My father sometimes took me fishing when I was a young boy. We would leave the house just before dawn, drive to a pond connected to a nearby river, park the car, carry our equipment to a little row boat and take off. For the next hours we would sit quietly in the boat, me putting worms on the hook and my father throwing the line in the water. I was not allowed to speak. Angling thus became a sport I didn't really like. Being an 8-year-old and holding my tongue for three to four hours was not easy, especially when words were an important tool for me to express myself – already being an 'editor' at our primary school newspaper!

When I grew up I decided not to pay any attention to the sport of fishing. Only when I started travelling to Scotland many years later was my interest rekindled, albeit professionally from the viewpoint of a writer and photographer. I remember when it all started. It was after a talk with John Grant and his wife Ishbel, owners of Glenfarclas. We were having lunch in a cosy fisherman's hotel in Aberlour, called the Dowans. The walls were crowded with stuffed salmon of enormous proportions and John remarked that there would be a contest the next day in the River Spey. Ishbel, being an avid angler herself, would participate. I decided to investigate and the next day I spent a very agreeable time talking to various contestants and taking photographs. One of the older fishermen told me an interesting story, connected to the Speyburn distillery, further upstream past the little town of Glenrothes.

According to the man, Speyburn would give you a bottle of single malt for free if you caught a salmon and put it back in the river to sustain wildlife. In order to prove that you really did, you needed a ghillie as a witness. For those unfamiliar with this typically Scottish phenomenon here is some clarification. A gillie or ghillie originally was the attendant of a Highland clan chief. Today it is a man or boy who attends someone on a hunting or fishing expedition. Etymologically the word stems from the Gaelic 'gille' meaning 'lad' or 'servant.' According to the Apple online Dictionary: 'The word was also found in the term *gilliewetfoot*, denoting a servant who carried the chief over a stream, used as a contemptuous name by Lowlanders for the follower of a Highland chief.' The term also applies to a special type of shoe used for Scottish country dancing – the ghillie brogue. Instead of digressing here into shoe fashion, let's turn back to the distillery.

Speyburn was built in 1897 by the Hopkins brothers, who at the time also owned Tobermory on the Isle of Mull. The famous architect Charles Doig designed the distillery. Ten years later Speyburn was scooped up by the Distillers Company Ltd, on its way to becoming the largest player in the Scottish whisky industry, culminating in Diageo about a century later. DCL kept Speyburn for 50 years and sold it to Scottish Malt Distillers in 1962. The new owner decided to close the drum maltings on the premises and started to buy malted barley from the commercial maltsters in 1968.

In 1991 Inver House Distillers took over the distillery and still owns it today, albeit that Inver House itself has been owned by Thai Beverage PCL since 2006. ThaiBev under its arm International Beverage Holdings Limited also owns the Knockdhu, Balblair, Balmenach and Old Pulteney distilleries.

Speyburn was first produced on 15 December 1897, the diamond jubilee year of Queen Victoria. To guarantee that the first whisky was indeed distilled in time, the employees worked all night long in a windowless still house whilst a mean snowstorm was raging outside. Legend has it that they produced one butt that night (approximately 600 litres).

Speyburn single malt is readily available as a 10-year-old and very affordable. In 2009 the distillery released the un-aged Bradan Orach. This Gaelic name means 'golden salmon.' It is a nice and friendly dram, in line with the beautiful surroundings of the distillery. Charles Doig outdid himself in 1897 since Speyburn today is a popularly photographed distillery in Scotland. The location is idyllic indeed but has an eerie story to it, told to me by friends who used to live in a house on the hill overlooking the distillery. Once a gallows stood there, also known as the gibbet. Our friends claim that they could hear the sound of the hatch dropping during quiet nights. In fact, The Gibbet is the distillery's nickname.

The fresh spring water for Speyburn comes from the Granty Burn, one of the larger tributaries of the Spey River. On that day when I went to the river Spey to watch the contestants catching salmon after salmon, I was lucky to capture one myself, albeit it with my camera. One young man struggled for about 15 minutes with the beastie and then held a magnificent example up in the air. I asked him whether he was going to collect his bottle of whisky at Speyburn but he declined. 'Goes on the barbecue tonight,' he smiled and walked back to his spot on the river.

At the end of the day, a case of a certain malt whisky appeared, seemingly out of nowhere. That night a whole group of anglers ate grilled salmon marinated with Speyburn on the banks of the river Spey. I was invited, too - an offer I couldn't refuse. Since then I have viewed fishing from a different angle!

Off the Beaten Track

We're back in Europe, after having had a beautiful four months stay in Charleston, during which time I succeeded in writing a first draft of a book on *Whisky & Jazz*. Thanks to our friend Deneen Bell we were introduced to jazz historian Jack McCray who offered his help in assessing the manuscript. On top of it all a respected Charlestonian book publisher took a liking to some of our books and considered publishing them in the US. What more can a writer wish?

The Whisky Couple flew back in a happy mood, along a beaten track. I've done the Atlantic crossing so many times since the early 1990s that we sometimes joke underway: 'Ah, we are at wave 249 already, lots of tail wind.' Only visiting Scotland outnumbers my transatlantic trips. The greater part of that country is well known to me although it still has hidden gems.

One of my favourite places in Scotland is Cape Wrath, on the most northwest tip of the Scottish mainland. It is even possible to go a little further west with Keodale ferry to the lighthouse, unmanned and operated fully automatically. From Cape Wrath, one has a magnificent view of the Kyle of Durness, a sea loch influenced heavily by the tide, and Ben Spionnaidh, the mountain of which I took a beautiful picture in 1995 during my first visit to this incredible place. An enlargement is framed, hanging on the wall of my study. I call it 'my mountain' and often look at it for inspiration.

When my son Sietse graduated from high school in 2005, I asked him what he wanted for a present: 'One week with you alone, in Scotland.' he answered, filling my heart with joy. I had travelled with him and his younger brother Melle through Scotland five years earlier. Sietse immediately fell in love with the country.

I thought it a nice idea to show Sietse my mountain and proposed to travel up north, where he hadn't been yet. It would give me the opportunity to make another picture of that mountain, 10 years older now. I imagined it wouldn't have changed much, but it was the idea that counted. The surface stone in that part of the world is over 2 billion years old and it is so sparsely inhabited that it seems nothing has altered during all those countless millennia. When we arrived however, the sky was clouded and my mountain hidden in the mist. Waiting and watching for the mountain to unveil itself, we found ourselves staring at a lonely otter swimming in the Kyle. As soon as he noticed us, he started to play hide and seek between some little rocks. We sat there for hours, talking and contemplating – this time of year it is still bright at 11 pm on Cape Wrath – before we returned to the hotel. The following morning I had to do with a partly mist-covered mountain but got my picture.

Our next stop would be the Highlander Inn in Craigellachie where we'd meet up with some old friends. From Cape Wrath it is a mere 160 miles south but a day's journey because of the mostly single-track roads with passing places now and then. The rugged and largely uninhabited Northern Highlands offer spectacular panoramas and they evoked sweet memories from earlier visits. Rounding Loch Eribol I chose a little by-road following Loch Hope, to rejoin the A836 at Altnaharra after 20 miles, continuing in southerly direction. Assuming I would know the way by head from this point we did away with the map (Sietse is a good navigator, by the way). Distracted by the lively conversation in the car I missed a turn and we suddenly found ourselves in uncharted territory. In a small village called Edderton, Sietse pointed to the left, 'A red brick chimney Dad, which distillery is that?' I blushed and had to confess I wasn't sure. 'Let's check it out.' Five minutes later we drove through the gate of Balblair, a

tiny delightful Northern Highland distillery, one of the few whose history goes back to the late 18th century.

In 2013 there would be a beautiful visitor centre added, but that was not the case in 2005. It looked deserted. When we started to take out our cameras a tall Scot came out of the door of the distillery office and gently asked what the purpose of our visit was. 'My father is a whisky writer', Sietse proudly announced, 'we need some pictures'. The man smiled and introduced himself as Gordon Bruce, production manager, and invited us to come inside. The distillery itself was silent for a couple of weeks, due to maintenance. 'I can take you around, but you have to wear a helmet inside the buildings', Gordon said.

It's always interesting to walk through a non-producing distillery, especially without any other visitors around. You can peek inside an empty still (yes, we enjoy even that) and take a really close look at all the equipment. Balblair is a traditional distillery, partly unchanged since it was built in 1790. Some of the warehouses date back to those early days. Entering the still house we noticed something special. Behind the pair that makes Balblair when in production stood a third, smaller one, covered in dust. 'We haven't used it since 1970', explained Gordon, 'we call it The Wee One.'

After having spent more than an hour in the distillery, during which time Gordon quietly answered all questions Sietse fired at him, we walked back to the little office where we were offered a vertical tasting, various vintages of the same single malt. The line-up was impressive: 10, 16, 24, 27, 38 and 40 years old. An excellent opportunity to experience how one whisky develops in the cask over a longer period of time. Sietse wrote his first 'professional' tasting note in my almanac: 'fresh, full but mild, robust and full of variety'.

Whereas Sietse took a liking to the 27-year-old, I preferred the 38, matured in ex-sherry casks. A stupendous whisky. Alas a limited bottling that is hard to get nowadays. The 16-year-old is a perfect dram for daily use, but also hard to get, since Balblair changed its line-up in 2007 and currently carries vintages. When we'd finished assessing the range, Gordon poured us a surprise dram. 'It's a 13-year-old', he smiled, 'something of an oddball.' I cautiously nosed and tasted with the tip of my tongue. 'Must be a stray cask, it is totally out of sync with the rest', I sighed. 'Lots of peat, Hans. Actually it was 4 stray casks, blended together'. I rinsed my mouth with water and reverently finished the 38-year-old. A chance too good to just let it pass.

'Will we make it to Craigellachie today, Dad?' Sietse looked a little concernedly at the empty glasses on the table in front of us. 'No son, we'll find a B&B for the night and travel further down south tomorrow.'

When we left the parking lot, Gordon waved his arm in farewell. That night we slept like babies in Edderton, in a lovely cottage along a not so beaten track.

Fast forward to 2016. Balblair was renovated thoroughly in 2007, after which a whole new series of vintages was launched in new stunning packaging. The first three of the series were from 1987, 1989 and 1997. Gordon Bruce went to Knock Dhu Distillery, on the fringe of the Speyside, owned by the same company. He now produces beautiful single malts under the brand name An Cnoc. In 2013 Balblair distillery was to become one of the locations for Ken Loach's road movie on whisky, called *The Angels' Share*.

And what about Sietse? After his studies at Utrecht University and The Hague College he joined the Edrington Group and worked as a brand ambassador for The Macallan, Highland Park and The Famous Grouse in the Netherlands for the last five years. March 2016 he was appointed European Brand Ambassador for The Macallan. I can assure you his tasting notes are bit more elaborate now.

Travels without Becky

One of my favourite authors is John Steinbeck. His monumental books *The Grapes of Wrath* and *East of Eden* are etched in my memory, along with little gems like *Of Mice and Men*, *Cannery Row* and *The Winter of Our Discontent*. In 1962 Steinbeck published a travel story titled *Travels with Charley*, an account of a long journey he undertook with his French poodle Charley and a camper truck named Rocinante (after Don Quixote's horse). He wanted to see his country one more time, knowing he was seriously ill.

A few years ago I returned to Europe after a prolonged stay in the USA. While waiting at Amsterdam Schiphol Airport for my luggage, I noticed a little man with greying hair and spectacles, standing next to me at the belt. I looked again and recognised Geert Mak, a well-known Dutch author of historical books. We engaged in a conversation and soon Steinbeck was the topic. At that time I did not know Mak had returned from a research trip for his upcoming book *Travels without John*. In this hefty tome he dissects the journey Steinbeck undertook a half century ago. Mak and his wife Mietsie followed Steinbeck's trail. He likes to travel with his spouse.

So do I. On my many travels, Becky usually accompanies me. It is really rare that she won't join me, and if that happens, the trip doesn't take more than a few days.

Not that one time, in May 2013, when I undertook a 10-day fieldtrip to Scotland with Marcel Langedijk, the leading lifestyle journalist of The Netherlands. He wanted to know more about whisky and, literally, follow *my* trail. To honour Geert Mak and John Steinbeck, I decided to write a travelogue of that trip and publish the first part in the Dutch whisky magazine *Whisky Passion*. Four more parts followed in the online version of WP. This is the first time that the entire story appears in print, in English. However, this tale does not commence in The Netherlands, but ... in New York, and without a dog!

The first time I met Marcel Langedijk was in 2009, during the launch of a 50-year-old Highland Park, in the Brandy Library in New York. That's where he revealed to me he didn't know much about whisky and wished to visit Scotland and its distilleries some time. Back in Europe we lost sight of each other and went our own ways – out of sight, out of mind. Until the turn of 2012, when we accidentally ran into each other at a lifestyle event in Amsterdam. 'Now it's gonna happen', we cried in unison. And what better opportunity to get Marcel acquainted with Scotland than the Spirit of Speyside Festival, celebrating its 14th year in 2013. For me it is a tradition and a reunion. Until today I have not missed one edition of the famed whisky fest.

I set up an itinerary taking us through a large part of Scotland in 10 days. I contacted various distillery managers I had befriended over the years and with the help of a couple of Dutch whisky importers made sure it would be a very special trip indeed. So here's our adventure on the road, written as a diary. It may serve as a guide for those who want to undertake a similar quest. Fasten your seatbelts; here we go, in reporter style!

Wednesday 1 May
Marcel arrives at our house at noon, driving a brand new Audi A6 Quattro All Road 3.0 Something. 'You're doing well, my friend', I remark and raise an eyebrow. 'No, Hans, I approached the importer and he suggested we take this beasty for a spin in Scotland, as long as we shoot some fine pictures in the Highlands for a fancy car magazine.' Hey, the tremendous advantages of travelling with a guy who has lifestyle

(figuratively) tattooed on his forehead. After lunch Becky waved us goodbye and we headed for IJmuiden to catch the ferry to Newcastle.

Thursday 2 May

After a quiet 18-hour crossing and a delightful breakfast we smoothly roll off the ferry around 9:30 am. Usually it takes an hour or more, but DFDS has given us a special badge with 'journalists' on it and we are given priority to leave the ship. We need that extra time since we are expected that same evening at the opening Gala of the Spirit of Speyside Festival, and we have a long way to go. Since a number of years it is 'en vogue' to host the evening at a particular distillery and this year it is The Glenlivet's turn. If you are pressed for time and want to speed up, which is fairly easy in this 'beastie', it is best to drive via Jedburgh to Edinburgh, take the Firth of Forth Bridge, adjacent to the famous railway bridge built by Thomas Telford, continue to Perth and then take the A9, direction Inverness.

It is a gorgeous route, taking you along Pitlochry, a stone's throw from the small, picturesque distillery of Edradour. We don't have time for a visit and tour, but do stop at nearby Moulin Inn, to have lunch and a nice pint of real ale. This is supposedly the oldest pub in Scotland and worth a stop. The ales on tap are locally brewed, behind the Inn. The brewery is open to the public.

After lunch we continue our route and follow the A9, via the Drumochter Pass, where Dalwhinnie distillery stands lonely but proud with a backdrop of snow-capped mountains. Past Aviemore we turn onto the A95 and head direction Elgin. A half hour later we enter the beautiful town of Grantown-on-Spey where, roughly 25 years ago, I first stood in the River Spey, barefooted, scooping up a handful of the crystal clear water that feeds so many distilleries.

And further we drive, until we reach the village of Craigellachie, my home from home in Scotland. We check into our rooms in the hotel and change into formal gear rapidly. General manager Kevin Smith offers to drive us to The Glenlivet Distillery, a mere half hour from the hotel. When we arrive at the distillery, we are welcomed with a whisky cocktail in the new still house, opened by Prince Charles in 2010. I see many familiar Scottish faces and introduce Marcel to as many people as possible. Various Dutch guests arrive, recidivists who have attended previous editions of the festival. Marcel looks at one of the large copper pot stills for the first time in his life and whispers in awe: 'Are we going to see more of that stuff?' An employee motions us to follow her to a temporarily emptied warehouse. 'Plenty to come, Marcel', I answer; I have not told him what we will encounter the next week and a half.

The warehouse has been converted into a gigantic restaurant that can seat the 300 people who were lucky to get a ticket. Ushers show guests to their tables. Mind you, this gala is so popular that it is sold out within two hours after the ticket sales goes online on the festival's website at a whopping £120 per person.

We are invited and guided to one of the tables in the front, as special guests of The Glenlivet. My lady hostess for the evening is Ann Miller, who has been working for The Glenlivet for a considerable time and is a well-known guest at various whisky festivals in Europe. We've known each other for years and always enjoy each other's company.

Between speeches and awards given to various people, we are presented with a three-course menu, each course accompanied by a different single malt. As a starter we enjoy a terrine of salmon with a 12-year-old Strathisla; the main course is lamb chops with Aberlour A'bunadh and the dessert a killer chocolate mousse with the pièce de resistance of the evening: a The Glenlivet from 1969, the year Woodstock was held. A quick look at Marcel informs me that he is already 'totally in love with single malt'. He is engaged in a lively discussion with the CEO of Pernod-Ricard. This French drinks company owns many distilleries, among which the aforementioned.

Shortly after midnight the party is over. The guests slowly make their way to the exit, dripping out of the warehouse like the last bit of alcohol from the spirit safe. Outside busses and taxis are on standby to take them home or to their hotel. Our taxi isn't there yet. We wait for 10 minutes. It is getting colder in the glen of the Livet and Marcel is more of a nice-weather-guy. With clattering teeth he asks if anybody will actually show up. After 20 minutes I slowly start to worry, but then Ann Miller shows up like a guardian angel and invites us to join her in her taxi and has the driver make a detour via the Craigellachie Hotel. When we arrive and get out of the car, waving goodbye to Ann, Marcel remarks: 'Everybody knows you here, don't they?' I respond, grinning: 'Well, they should, after 25 years.'

Friday 3 May
We get up early with a hearty breakfast in our stomachs and cross the river Spey, turn left direction Archiestown and arrive at Easter Elchies Estate five minutes later – the home of The Macallan. We've been offered a complete estate tour and will be hosted by Margaret Gray and Morag Ralph, whom I joined on a ghost hunt at the distillery grounds many years and festivals ago (as you can read in *The Road to Craigellachie Revisited*). When we park the Audi in front of the main house, Marcel quietly asks: 'So it's here that you have your own cask of whisky?' I nod and promise we will have a look at it before we leave.

During the festival it gets rather busy with visitors who

want to take tours, so Margaret arranged to show us around before the crowds arrive. It seems we have the distillery to ourselves, the coming hour at least. My travel companion can't have a better tour guide, since Margaret's father worked for the Macallan. It's in the blood so to speak. Who wants to know more about maturation and wood, should really take this tour. It's so well explained and displayed. After our tour it is time to inspect my cask. It's been lying in a warehouse on the estate for more than four years now and I can vividly remember the day Becky and I filled it with new make spirit, after which I singlehandedly rolled the barrel to the warehouse. When the whisky is 12 years old we will commence bottling it.

The cask looks fine, and I had not expected otherwise. After a short interview with distillery manager Russell Anderson we walk back to Easter Elchies house where Morag takes over with a Landrover to drive us around the estate. We make our first stop at a small, wooden fishing cottage, where those who can afford it may try to catch some salmon from the river Spey. The Macallan is the only distillery in Scotland who owns fishing rights covering about two miles of Spey. We are allowed to give it a try and an experienced ghillie shows us how to properly use a fly rod. At first we make a total mess of it and are rapidly becoming the laughing stock of the spectators, all experienced in the craft. After a little while, we do manage to operate the equipment properly, but no catch of the day.

We drive along and notice small green sprouts in a field nearby. In months to come they will grow into rows of Minstrel barley. The Macallan proudly grows part of the barley needed on its own estate.

Morag offers us lunch in the Highlander Inn, on the opposite side of the Spey, where her husband Richard joins us. Becky and I have been friends with them for some time. Once

they visited us for a culinary event in my Dutch hometown Zwolle, as part of a Scottish delegation. The dress code was festive, and Richard appeared to have forgotten his kilt. It was the only occasion thus far that I could actually lend one of my own kilts to a Scotsman. We still laugh about it, each time we see one another.

Marcel observes, nods his head and takes photographs. After lunch we stop for a short visit at the Fiddichside Inn, the smallest pub in Scotland. The publican Joe, in his mid 80s now, still is the perfect host in this iconic tiny and cosy place. Then we head back to the Craigellachie Hotel where we savour a few drams in the world-famous Quaich Bar and enjoy a simple but tasty meal in the restaurant.

Saturday 4 May
A cup of coffee at a castle. That doesn't happen to me every day. And surely not at a castle that has been occupied by the same family for more than four centuries. I met Lady Clare Russell Grant-McPherson for the first time in 2000 when I was in Speyside to make a documentary on whisky for Dutch television. I was looking for a beautiful backdrop and she allowed me to use Ballindalloch Castle. In 2012 we jointly opened a Scottish Food Fair in the Craigellachie Hotel. After the fair she told me: 'Please come and visit us the next time you are in the vicinity.' Well, you don't refuse a lady's request. Not at all when you are dealing with the Lord Lieutenant of Banffshire.

Visiting the Russells, as they call themselves, is an excellent opportunity for Marcel to witness a part of the life of the Scottish landed gentry. Apart from that Lady Clare has successfully published a couple of cooking books, which interests Marcel as well.

We load up The Beast, as we decided to call the Audi henceforth, and head for Ballindalloch Castle, a 20-minute drive. We've been given directions to take the back entrance and may park our car in front of the gorgeous buildings.

Lady Clare's husband Oliver Russell quietly walks to our car, bids us a cordial welcome and invites us inside to have coffee and biscuits in the cosy living room. The couple enthusiastically tells us about new plans for Ballindalloch Estate. A few years ago Laird Oliver had a golf course laid out, open to whoever wants to play a round of golf. 'When you have land and you live in Scotland, you just have to have a golf course,' he explains in a friendly but serious voice, when we take his four-wheel drive around the links. Coming from him, it only sounds logical. He emphasises the fact that no membership is needed. 'Everybody should be able to play here', he smiles.

Do they enjoy whisky? Marcel wants to know. 'Clare's great-grandfather founded Cragganmore Distillery nearby. It's in the blood'. In 2015 the Russells would open their own Ballindalloch Distillery next to the golf course. But that is another story, for another book. The castle itself is partly open to the public at specific hours. So are the beautiful gardens in the surrounding woodlands. Upon returning to the castle I present Lady Clare with a copy of *A Taste of Whisky*, a favour returned with one of her own cooking books, with a special dedication for Becky. 'Please bring her the next time', she says and accompanies us outside to wave us goodbye, together with Oliver.

'Where now, Sir Hanselot?' says Marcel, who, after our visit at the castle, decides to give me that moniker and will continue to use it ever after. 'Well, you've seen a few distilleries that have been around for a while and were modernized fairly recently. What about a real oldie?'

Those in the know immediately realise I want to take Marcel to Strathisla, the oldest working distillery in this part of Scotland, founded in 1786. We take the A95 to Keith and follow the signs to the distillery, which is one of the most picturesque on the planet and probably the most photographed as well.

After having visited the streamlined new still houses of The Glenlivet and The Macallan, there is no better contrast for us than a tour at Strathisla. The water wheel that supplied energy in times past still has a prominent place in front of the two pagoda-topped kilns. The layout of the distillery is not quite a showcase of logistical efficiency, but that is part of the charm of this gem from Pernod Ricard's stable. The man in charge of tours is Boa Andersson, a chemist from Sweden who once visited Scotland out of curiosity, and then decided to stay. It is a pleasure to hear him explain. He combines a surplus of knowledge with a passion for the product. Since the afternoon is entirely ours, with no other appointments made, I accept his offer for a vertical tasting. Soon we are comfortably seated in the VIP room in the visitor centre, some enticing cask samples in front of us. Since Strathisla doubles as the Spiritual Home of the deluxe blend Chivas, the attention to detail is astounding. Not only the tasting room but also the shop is a pleasure to the eye. Everything breathes grandeur without becoming suffocating. On the contrary, this place is designed to make you feel at ease. Boa in the meantime continues to lecture us on the finer aspects of the cratur. The last sample in the flight is a special one from the long silent Glenugie distillery – bottled at cask strength, a vintage from the 1980s listening to the name *Deoch an Doras* (in the local Doric dialect, this translates as 'one for the road'.)

When we load up The Beast with a case of Strathisla Single Malt, Boa stares admiringly at the car. You can almost hear him think 'Do writers and journalists earn so much that they can afford to drive a car worth more than £100,000?' I clarify for him how we got the car and he immediately responds: 'May I take a picture?' We take a few ourselves, with him, the car and the distillery in the background, promising to send them via email later in the week. With a big smile on his face he waves us goodbye, until we round the corner, out of sight.

Via Keith we take the A96 in the southeasterly direction making a short stop in Huntly to visit the famous whisky shop of independent bottler Duncan Taylor. Then we continue our journey for the day and turn left, just before the village of Colpy, onto the A920. This road takes us to our next destination – Meldrum House Hotel in the village Old Meldrum. My indestructible and dear Scottish agent Lesley Ann Parker arranged two nights with dinner for us. This is a fine hotel and the food as well as chef are at least one Michelin star worthy. The surrounding golf course is a beauty and a challenge at the same time. In short, an environment much to the liking of a lifestyle journalist and a whisky writer. Especially since the village harbours another distillery – old Glen Garioch, also founded at the end of the 18th century. It is too late for a visit. Instead we enjoy a splendid four-course dinner, take a nightcap in the bar, which is hewn out of a rock, and go to bed. That night I dream about finally making that hole-in-one. Unfortunately there is no witness.

Sunday 5 May
Ah, Glen Garioch is not open on Sundays. Many distilleries currently produce 24/7 to keep up with demand, but this honourable lady from 1797 chooses to keep a day of rest. The single malt produced here is not well known, but slowly gaining appreciation with a larger crowd of whisky aficionados. The distillery belongs to a group of distilleries owned by the Japanese drinks company Suntory. Glen Garioch is the most easterly located commercial distillery of the country and worth a visit. We have to be satisfied with taking a few pictures outside, on a silent but sunny Sunday afternoon. I

don't mind too much since half a year ago I had an extensive visit with my son Sietse.

Although Glen Garioch is not part of the Speyside distilleries, lying too far to the east, under the smoke of Aberdeen, distance-wise a visit can easily be undertaken during the Spirit of Speyside Festival. The old malting floors and the kiln are decommissioned but open to the public. A beautiful cast iron spiral staircase leads up to the kiln floor. I consider Glen Garioch a must see for the true whisky lover.

Around 2 pm we have to be back in Craigellachie to attend an auction of whisky bottles and paraphernalia. It's one of the more than 130 events during the five-day Spirit of Speyside Festival. There is something to do for everyone, which makes this festival so nice.

To show Marcel a bit more of the natural surroundings we don't return via Huntly, but instead choose the B9002 direction Gartly and follow the Cabrach to end up in Dufftown where we turn at the distinctive square clock tower back to Craigellachie. The village hall has been the location for the auction since years. Marcel is astonished to see how much is being paid for certain bottles. The complete Flora & Fauna series, 26 bottles in total, goes for a whopping £3,600. In itself not too bad, but far too much for a modest whisky writer, who prefers to collect packaging, anecdotes and stories instead of whisky anyway. The auctioneer donates his entire provision to charity. We're talking a couple of thousands pounds here!

After a farewell dram with Lesley in the Quaich Bar at the Craig, where I keep my own bottle for special occasions, we drive back to Meldrum House Hotel. This time we leave the menu for what it is and walk into the village. Marcel wants to try a little restaurant he googled earlier that day. It is of the Thai persuasion and named Tiger Lilly. Yes, a Thai in this part of Scotland, really, and the food is great. The second night in the golf resort hotel I don't hit a ball, but sleep like a log.

Monday 6 May

Today we have to drive quite a bit. Our first goal is Alness, where Dalmore Distillery awaits us on the beautiful shore of the Cromarty Firth. The route is easy, just follow the A97 westbound until you reach Inverness and then keep the A9 in northerly direction. Don't take the first Alness exit, but continue. Soon you will see a sign pointing in the direction of Dalmore.

Upon our arrival a whole herd of German whisky lovers occupies the grounds, but they are already on their way to the tour bus that had taken them to the distillery at an early hour. They are done and the distillery is ours. An arrangement beforehand, organised by brand manager Caroline Kroef at Dutch importer A Brand New Day.

This time we are welcomed by Shauna Jennens, in daily life Distillery Ambassador for Dalmore. After a short tour, where we admire the unique pot stills with their flat heads and cooling jackets (a rarity in the industry), she invites us for lunch in the boardroom.

The Dalmore presents itself as the ultimate luxury whisky and illustrates this with the Constellations Series, which is extremely rare and expensive. Fortunately Dalmore also caters to those with a smaller purse. The 12 and 15-year-old versions are tasty and affordable. The 18 and the Alexander III are stunners too, but in a different price bracket. Shauna offers us a 30-year-old Dalmore Ceti. I am used to some pretty good and astonishing single malts, after having professionally tasted whisky for more than 25 years, but this one blows me away. Incredible, a succulent tropical fruit basket, not a trace of wood. Marcel quickly realises this is not a daily dram and takes time to enjoy the amber liquid. Shauna appreciates our enjoyment.

Then it is time to visit the small but well-stocked shop. Marcel picks up a bottle of the Dalmore Cigar Malt. During lunch he told Shauna about his passion for cigars and his recent visit to Cuba and Nicaragua. He plans to write a book about cigars (eventually I would end up translating that book into English in 2016, appropriately called *Cigaragua*). I choose a special release, only for sale at the distillery. 'Excellent choice', Shauna laughs and refuses any payment for both bottles. 'Consider it a gift, gentlemen! When we leave the parking lot, Marcel sighs: 'How on earth did you arrange that, Sir Hanselot?' I just smile silently and drive on.

We now head south to Loch Ness, waiting for Marcel, dark, deep, cold, luring, mysterious. Still enjoying the fantastic visit at The Dalmore, I steer The Beasty below Alness to Dingwall and follow the A862 in southern direction. Ay, ay, in Muir of Ord stands Glen Ord, a distillery we can't refuse. Especially since they have their own maltings, which gives me an opportunity to explain to Marcel a bit more about that part of the process. 'Can you take another?' I carefully ask. 'All right Sir Hanselot, one more to mark for the day.'

Since the visitor centre was refurbished I have not been here and welcome the renewed acquaintance. We arrive without the staff having prior knowledge and therefore have to settle for the standard whisky tourist tour, something Marcel has to experience, in order to get the full picture. No disappointment here, the tour guide is one of the funniest I have encountered in 25 years. A true Scot with a nose like a strawberry and a terrific sense of humour, well injected, without being overbearing or damaging the transfer of knowledge about the process.After 45 minutes we are on the road again, continuing on the A862 and turning left upon the A863 direction Drumnadrochit, arriving a good 20 minutes later. This village with the interesting name not only is famous for its extensive Nessie exhibition, but also because of the Fiddler Inn, four times chosen as the Best Whisky Bar of Scotland. An accomplishment not to be underestimated.

Proprietor Jon Beach had invited me at Maltstock in 2011 to come visit, but I had not found time to do so. Hence, it was a first one for both Marcel and I. The Inn has various rooms and it is a simple but comfortable place to spend the night. We parked The Beasty opposite the Fiddler and crossed the street. Inside Jon, with a broad smile on his bearded face, welcomes us with an already poured dram 'Your own Springbank Blues Edition, Hans.' Well, to start the evening with one of your own bottlings is not a bad way to get into some serious dramming.

The walls of the Fiddler Inn are adorned with a huge number of bottles, whiskies known, unknown, rare, readily available, affordable, expensive, you name it. This appropriately named Whisky Library is the brainchild of Jon's father Dick Beach, who started collecting whiskies in Inverness. When he moved to Drumnadrochit there was no room to store them, so father and son decided to use the bottles as 'wallpaper' and make the contents available to customers.

Hardly have I touched my Springbank, when a hand descends on my shoulder. I turn around and look straight into the smiling face of an old friend, the Scottish painter Ian Gray, who designed the labels for my future Macallan bottling. Those who do not have heard of him: he paints distilleries and landscapes in a very distinctive and recognisable style. And whoever decides to share a dram with him, better have a lot of time at his or her disposal, and needs to hold his or her liquor well.

We all sit down and Jon puts a few interesting bottles on the table. After a while Marcel leaves for a moment. I immediately grab the opportunity. 'Guys, it's his maiden trip to Scotland. What about baptising him in Loch Ness tonight?'

'Midnight, at the ruins of Urquhart Castle. I'll drive.', Jon replies and refrains from drinking more. Marcel returns, totally unaware of what is going to happen in a few hours. When the clock strikes 12, we grab our intrepid lifestyle guru by the arms and throw him in the back of Jon's Landrover, driving in the pitch black night to the designated spot, a mere 10 minutes away. 'What's happening?' Marcel demands to know. 'You will be baptised', we yell simultaneously, while Ian's girlfriend Biggy keeps a bottle of whisky and glasses at hand. 'In Loch Ness!'

Marcel shivers at the thought and wishes he was back in Cuba. It is cold, dangerously cold when we arrive at the loch. Actually too dangerous to go in completely. 'Only as far as your ankles', I try to calm Marcel down. He looks at me like a dog that has lost its precious bone. 'All right, I'll walk with you into the lake', I promise magnanimously. My offer is much appreciated by our esteemed friends, who yell war cries to encourage us to get into the ice-cold water. Within a minute we're both in and out of the water. I have never longed for a dram as much as that night. The brave are honoured with a glass of that beautiful, deeply smoky Lagavulin Distillers Edition. From now on Sir Hanselot will call Marcel Langedijk 'Lord Ness'.

Tuesday 7 May

It's impossible to see the whole of Scotland in ten days, especially with so many stops underway, places where great whiskies are produced and consumed. Scotland's nature is so overwhelming and diverse that choosing one route automatically rules out another equally beautiful way to go.

Back in The Netherlands I already had promised Marcel to show him some really dramatic scenery when in Scotland. Today is the day for it. We plan to drive through Glen Coe, the glen of weeping. We need to go in a southerly direction

anyway, as golfing and whisky paradise Gleneagles awaits us. We are supposed to sample a new range in the Johnnie Walker series, followed by a grand dinner in the one Michelin star restaurant. But, time is on our side; we are not expected until five pm.

We say our goodbyes to Jon and his father Dick, who in my opinion somewhat resembles a Scottish version of Ernest Hemingway, and take the western shore of Loch Ness. The A82 leads us to Fort William, at the foot of Ben Nevis, the highest mountain of Great Britain. The sun caresses the snow-capped mountain ridge and we park the car at a panoramic viewpoint to enjoy the scenery. On and on we go, along Loch Linnhe. Marcel is truly amazed by the views and wishes his dad were with us to see all this natural beauty. We're lucky; the skies are blue with some white clouds chasing each other. The weather gods take a liking to us today. Passing Ballachulish we see Glen Coe looming in the distance. In the car I told Marcel the horrendous story of the Campbells who massacred their hosts the MacDonalds after having feasted for a fortnight on their expense. They were ordered by the government to do so, in the early morning of 13 February 1692. The Campbells and the MacDonalds never got along after that bloody event.

The A82 becomes more and more narrow, at least seemingly. In reality the mountains on either side of the road are rapidly approaching. Whether rain or shine, storm or snow, Glen Coe always makes you shiver. It is so impressive, such an unforgettable experience. Reaching the narrowest stretch in the glen, we park The Beasty and grab our cameras to immortalise the moment.

It feels like some kind of liberation when finally, at the end of the glen, Rannoch Moor opens in front of us. The scenery still takes our breath away and the sun does not disappoint us. In Crianlarich we turn left on the A85. It's time for lunch and Sir Hanselot knows a fine spot where Lord Ness can have a pint outside, with a grandiose view of the Falls of Dochart. Once upon a time I photographed a fisherman here who struggled with a huge salmon. Outside the Dochart Inn we enjoy a bowl of Cullen Skink with a real ale from a brewery in the vicinity of Killin. Life is good.

With our bellies full we return to the A85, and drive further south, via Lochearnhead, the eponymous loch and St Fillans. I stop at Earngrove Cottage to show Marcel where I wrote the greater part of my second novel. Ulla, the owner, is not at home, so we continue the road. In Comrie, the next village, we turn right on the B278. This is a beautiful tiny back road, its scenery compressing the whole of Scotland in one, ending in a T-junction, where we turn right again. A hundred yards later left onto an even tinier road, direction Auchterarder, where the famed Gleneagles Spa and Golf Resort is located.

Approaching from this side, you have to go around the resort, since the grand entrance is on the opposite end of the village. We enter through the gate and drive along a broad lane lined with trees, passing the golf links, the clubhouse and follow the directions to the hotel. No smiling Jon Beach and Ian Gray in well-worn jeans and T-shirts here, instead a stylishly uniformed porter who gesticulates to a valet who is to park The Beasty, after another footman has taken care of our luggage, stored them on a trolley and wheeled them inside. That too is Scotland, I love these contrasts. Culture and nature alike.

We check in and repair to our rooms, both having the size of a small ballroom. I take a shower in the spacious bathroom. Drying myself off, I glance out of the window and see Marcel in the distance, walking to a bench in the park-like gardens surrounding the hotel buildings. In front of him on a square lawn, a dog trainer busies himself with eight black Labradors. In a short while I join my companion and we walk to the clubhouse. We are to be entertained in the Blue Bar, built around Johnnie Walker Blue Label, by the amiable brand ambassador David Sinclair. He explains he once started at Gleneagles as a bartender but rose in the ranks to become a true ambassador of Johnnie Walker. He asks if we know Herman van der Mey in The Netherlands, his mirror image, work wise speaking. 'Of course.', we answer, 'Who doesn't know Herman?' and put the new Gold Reserve, the Platinum 18 and the Blue Label to the test. David is a fast talker with a true passion for quality blends. After some time we sadly have to interrupt his entertaining stories, since we are expected to show up in the Strathearn restaurant, whose chef has earned his spurs, or should I say, stars. 'Please give Herman my cordial greetings', David calls out as we leave the Blue Bar.

The dinner is art, pure art, delicious art. Hardly ever have I tasted such a succulent, but not too fatty, smoked salmon, cut to our liking at the table. For the occasion we switch from whisky to white wine. After all, we don't have to drive that far tomorrow. Edinburgh is only an hour away, notwithstanding a full schedule for the day to come.

Wednesday 8 May
'The only thing I did not arrange in The Netherlands, Lord Ness, is a hotel in Edinburgh', I casually remark, when turning off the Gleneagles estate onto the road. 'No problem, Sir Hanselot. Long live booking.com'. In five minutes Marcel has booked us online into a very affordable hotel – a 10-minute walk from the city centre of old Edinburgh, near Holyrood Park. It is called the Masson Hotel and it belongs to the university. I can surely recommend it. For only £60 each we both had a room, including breakfast. That is extremely affordable for the capital of Scotland. The rooms are simple, but

128

clean with a shower similar to those in the standard cabins of DFDS Seaways, the ferry that will ultimately bring us back to The Netherlands. The next morning we enjoy an excellent breakfast and walk at leisure through the city centre, each processing silently what we experienced in more than a week of travels. Our first stop in the city is Whiski, an award-winning pub on the Royal Mile, known for its succulent burgers. We order a pair and I introduce Lord Ness to a few of my favourite Scottish ales, among which Punk IPA from Brewdog in Fraserburgh. Ale with an Attitude!

After lunch we continue our walk on the Royal Mile direction Edinburgh Castle and enter Royal Mile Whiskies, a must see whisky shop when in town. Inside I encounter a young Dutch couple, planning to end their first trip to Scotland with the purchase of a special single malt. They are assisted by a knowledgeable shop employee but seem rather intimidated by the huge display of different whiskies. Understandable, but they will get their bottle in the end.

Not us, we have to continue. The Scotch Whisky Experience is waiting for us, on the other side of the street, close to the square in front of the castle. Lord Ness must ride in the motorised whisky cask, just as I once did in 1990 during my first visit to Edinburgh. I volunteer to come along and do not regret it. The diorama has been thoroughly modernised and is much more entertaining than I recall. But there is something else I really want to see here. A few years ago Diageo bought a unique collection of whisky bottles from an illustrious Brazilian collector, who had three demands before the collection changed hands. Firstly nobody would reveal the price paid, secondly the collection was not to be broken up and thirdly it should be on display where every interested whisky lover could see it. Diageo asked the Heritage Centre to permanently house the collection, which they did excellently. Visiting the Centre only for that collection is worthwhile, although they have more to offer.

The Amber Restaurant at the Centre offers a fine menu for the hungry traveller. Marketing Manager Julie Trevisan Hunter, who had arranged the visit, offers us a dram of a 25-year-old blended whisky, bottled for the Centre's upcoming 25th anniversary. 'Not on sale yet, so here is a true premier,' she kindly smiles, while explaining the growing role of her company as an educational centre for the industry. 'We offer various tours and staff of bars, hotels and restaurants are regularly trained here.' I realise I haven't paid any attention to the Centre in a long time and promise to do so. Here's some proof!

The clock ticks along and reminds us that it is time to go and visit the next venue on our schedule. The Scotch Malt Whisky Society (SMWS), of which I have been a member since 1990. They own two different venues in Edinburgh. One in Leith, a place I have frequented many times, and one on 28 Queen Street, a place I had not had the pleasure to visit yet. So that's where we are headed. The Dutch (!) manager Jan Willem Damen has offered us a five-course dinner with accompanying single malts. But first we will have a welcome dram in the members' bar upstairs. Soon I hear a familiar voice. When I turn around I meet the gaze of my dear friend Charles MacLean, chairman of the tasting panel of the SMWS. Ever congenial, he joins us, which gives Marcel the chance to meet the don among whisky writers, considered the world's leading Scotch whisky expert. After a while Charlie leaves in order to commence a tasting session below and we repair to the restaurant on the ground floor.

I have tasted many whisky and food combinations, even wrote a book about it, but what we are presented here is phenomenal. Never ever have I dined in Scotland so excellently when it comes to pairing dishes with the right single malts. The chef deserves a couple of stars, and so does the sommelier. All pairings form a seamless menu and all flavours are in perfect harmony. We unanimously agree and the pain is not in the paying. The price per menu is fair, £65 including the whiskies.

After the sumptuous meal we walk outside, utterly satisfied. My son Sietse gave us a tip for a good music venue so we head for the Jazz Bar at Chambers St for a nightcap and some great straight jazz. Our field trip nears its end. The next morning we have to leave Scotland and drive to Newcastle, in order to catch the ferry back home.

Thursday 9 May
Plenty of time, the ferry only leaves at five in the afternoon. Reserve at least four hours of travelling time from Edinburgh to North Shields, where the ferry is moored, and you can easily make it, even able to choose between different routes to get to Newcastle. 'Shall we visit one more distillery to say goodbye to Scotland?', I suggest to Lord Ness, who surrenders without any protest. The A68 leads us past Dalkeith where we turn left on the A6093. Signs with Glenkinchie Distillery point the way. I pre-arranged this visit. Still home, I'd made a phone call to Isobel Gardiner that we planned to visit Glenkinchie on May 9. Those who frequent the Dutch whisky festivals will know her. For years she was the 'mascot' for many, presenting Diageo's whiskies with fervour and passion, before she went into retirement. However, if some of her 'Dutch boys' want to come to the distillery, she is always happy to greet them with a cup of coffee. And I can tell you, many go yearly to see her. When driving from Newcastle up north along the A68, Glenkinchie will be the first distillery in Scotland you will encounter. It is a pretty one, and one of the very few in the Lowlands. One special artefact on display is a scale model of a whisky distillery, once built for the World Exhibition in 1900. It supposedly worked at the

time but fell into disrepair. Fortunately a former employee lovingly restored it for all visitors to see.

Isobel delights in seeing us. Another fine characteristic of Scotland. The huge engagement Scots show with their national drink. Honestly, they can never really retire from the whisky industry, and I don't think they ever want to. When we leave, Isobel hands me a packet. 'This is for Jock Shaw, please give it to him upon your return in The Netherlands. And give my greetings to Dennis and Ronald.' (long time Dutch whisky ambassadors).

'Let's go,' Marcel remarks, 'we also have to find a place to lunch before we reach Newcastle. This time I take the A7 to Galashiels, then it's Jedburgh with its imposing cathedral ruins and then the border country. We pass the monoliths that mark the border between Scotland and England. I always feel slightly melancholy at that point and I notice Marcel is a bit quiet, too. Half an hour later we park the Beasty in front of the Redesdale Arms, promoting itself with the moniker The First and Last Restaurant (before or after the border, whatever way the traveller arrives). The Fish 'n' Chips are a treat. Another good hour and a half and we see the ferry in the docks at North Shields, quietly waiting.

Friday 10 May
Lucky me. I've rarely experienced a rough passage on the waters between Newcastle and IJmuiden. Alas, last night it was gale force nine, and Sir Hanselot cannot cope very well with the crossing in any kind of weather. I do have pills and always take them, which helps, but this time I feel rather brackish when we arrive in the harbour of IJmuiden. And what about Marcel? How does he feel? He takes the steering wheel, with an immensely satisfied smile on his face. Lord Ness lost his heart in Scotland. I nod. Mission accomplished. Another soul saved. And a friend gained. Scotland unites!

The Whisky Island

That wonderful place on the southwest coast of Scotland, from where the mighty peated whiskies come with names like Laphroaig, Ardbeg and Lagavulin, complemented with their less peaty brothers Bruichladdich, Bunnahabhain, Bowmore, Caol Ila, Kilchoman, and last but not least, the very tasty peated blended Scotch Black Bottle. Let's go back to the dawn of time.

Scientists estimate the age of the earth at about 4.5 billion years. What now is known as Scotland originally was an enormous land mass called Laurentia, stretching out to Greenland and North America. Around 4.5 million years ago it collided with two other gigantic landmasses named Baltica and Avalonia, each consisting of different types of stone. As a result Scotland was divided along several fault lines, each with their own geological characteristics.

The Isle of Islay itself was formed some 60 million years ago after a long series of volcanic eruptions, albeit that some surface stones date back to half the age of the earth: at Portnahaven pebbles of Lewisian gneiss can be found in the little bay that is a natural shelter for seals.

The first traces of human habitation on Islay originated 10,000 years ago, after the last minor ice age. At the time the climate was milder and Islay would probably have been more wooded than today. Mesolithic fishers and hunters landed on the island by boat from the mainland. These nomadic people became settlers around 3500 BC, when the Neolithic period commenced. Evidence for that is found in remains of pottery and stone axes for felling trees.

When the farming population grew, the people started building burial tombs with cairns on top. These multi-chambered graves can be found in several places, most notably in

Port Charlotte and at Cragabus in The Oa. Standing stones started to appear at the end of the Neolithic period. The Cultoon Stone Circle, built between 2500-1500 BC might have been an early astronomical device. During this period the climate gradually changed to become wetter and colder. Moorlands developed and the heavy rainfall caused peat bogs.

In the Iron Age Islay was littered with small fortresses, being a battleground for many an armed argument. Stone hill forts like Dun Nosebridge in the Laggan Valley probably date back to 400 BC. Around this time Christianity came to Islay, brought by Irish monks like St Columba. They started to build little chapels everywhere, divided over tiny parishes with names like Kilnave and Kildalton (kil is derived from the Gaelic 'cill' meaning church), which each had their own burial ground. In the next couple of ages beautiful stone crosses were erected in the so-called Iona-tradition.

The Kildalton Cross, a fine example of this style, richly decorated with Celtic, Pictish, Northumbrian and Irish motifs, dates back to approximately 750 AD. Not long after the Viking raiders began to pester the Islay coast. The clergy retreated to Ireland and left the population to fend for itself. On the one hand the Norse and Danish intruders were extremely cruel. Excavations under the Kildalton Cross showed the remains of a body that was 'blood-eagled', a favourite pastime of the Vikings. A captive, usually a chief, would be tied to the ground on his belly. Then his lungs and heart were torn out and spread on his back. This horrible punishment was supposed to be an 'honour' only bestowed upon great warriors. On the other hand the Norse slowly mixed with the indigenous Christians and were converted themselves. Evidence of the presence of the Vikings can be found in burial grounds such as Cruach Mhor.

It is often said that the Ileachs truly differ from the Scots, which might have been caused by the fact that they were under Norse rule much longer than their Pictish and Scottish cousins on the mainland.

Halfway the 12th century the Norse yoke was finally thrown off the Ileach people's shoulders when Somerled, King of Argyll, defeated the Norse at sea. He founded the MacDonald clan and chose Dunyvaig Castle as his residence. The remains of this fortress can still be seen in Lagavulin Bay, a stone's throw from Laphroaig.

Around the turn of the 13th century, Angus Og, a descendant of Somerled, rose to power. His son John acquired the title Lord of the Isles in 1336. From that date the Clan MacDonald ruled not only over Islay, but also over the Kintyre peninsula, Knapdale, Skye, Lewis and the Western part of Scotland. The seat of power was moved to Finlaggan, Islay.

The Chiefs of Clan Donald chose Finlaggan at Eilean Mor, in the centre of the island, as the seat of power for the Lord of the Isles. The first Lord of the Isles was named Good John of Islay because he was a pious man and helped build many churches. His father Angus Og modified the Great Seal of Islay, which is shown on the label of a famous blended Scotch whisky, containing more than a sip of Laphroaig: Islay Mist. In 1542 the title 'Lord of the Isles' was seized by the English Crown and held ever since. The remains of the stronghold of Clan Donald can still be seen on Eilean Mor and are in the custody of the Finlaggan Trust.

The MacDonalds continued to rule this part of Scotland until 1542 when Donald Dubh (grandson of John II, the 4th Lord of the Isles) lost a rebellion. The Campbells of Cawdor seized power and eventually took Dunyvaig from the MacDonalds, who had owned the castle for more than 450 years.

In the early 17th century the Scottish king gave Islay

to Sir John Campbell of Cawdor, who managed to defeat the MacDonalds definitively a couple of years later. Islay would slowly become integrated into Scotland. The Cawdor Campbells weren't too successful in ruling Islay. They were hardly ever there and preferred to stay in Argyll. There was one exception to that rule, Sir Hugh Campbell, who erected Islay House around 1680. Eventually it became too big a burden to his successor John Campbell who ran into financial disaster and had to sell Islay to Daniel Campbell of the Shawfield branch of the clan.

The Shawfield Campbells brought great prosperity to Islay and were responsible for building many roads and villages such as Bowmore with its famous round church. When Daniel Campbell the Younger died in 1777, his brother Walter Campbell succeeded him from Skipness. The population grew from an estimated 5,000 in 1755 to more than 8,000 in 1802 when the first official census on Islay was held.

In 1816 Daniel Campbell's grandson Walter Frederick Campbell inherited Islay. He initiated many changes on the island, several of which were so influential that they can still be noted today, mainly in housing and farming. The population continued to prosper and grow until coming to a grinding halt around 1845, partly caused by overpopulation (15,000 inhabitants), partly by the potato disease from neighbouring Ireland. Clearances took place, forcing many people off the island. Walter Frederick Campbell faced a huge financial crisis and his affairs were handed to a Trust. His son John Francis Campbell dealt with the creditors and was assisted by John Ramsay, a local farmer and distiller. Finally, in 1853 Islay was sold to the extremely wealthy businessman James Morrison for £500,000. This purchase ended clan Campbell's ownership of Islay.

James Morrison already suffered bad health at the time he acquired Islay and left business in the hands of his sons

Alfred and Charles, the latter most prominently involved. John Ramsay managed to buy the Kildalton estate from the Morrisons in 1855, when they decided to sell limited parts of Islay. Charles Morrison died in his nineties. His nephew Hugh, son of Alfred, became the sole heir. Being married to a granddaughter of Walter Frederick Campbell, he coincidentally re-established a link to the Campbells of Shawfield.

The Morrison family sold off more parcels of their estate in years to come, but kept Islay House. In 1964, James Morrison's great-grandson John Granville Morrison was created Lord Margadale. Eventually the Morrisons sold Islay House in 1985. The current head of the family is Alistair John, 3rd Lord Margadale and still connected to the Campbells, via his great-grandmother.

At the height of its population, 15,000 people inhabited Islay. Beginning with the clearances in the mid 1850s the population slowly declined to today's number of approximately 3,500. The Ileachs share a surface of 61,956 hectares and eight distilleries (with plans for a ninth and maybe a tenth). Most estates that were once owned by the Campbells and made up all of Islay are now in the hands of a small group of wealthy individuals. However, one Campbell still reigns in a tiny part of Islay: Laphroaig's distillery manager John Campbell.

No.3 WASH
STILL CONTENTS
10500 ltrs.

EDINBURGH

The Making of *The Legend of Laphroaig*

Dentists and whisky form a great pair. Not only because novocaine will always lose its place to a single malt, at least where I come from, but also because I may reckon having at least two friends among them. Two that enjoy their whisky as well. The first one is my long-time buddy Rudolf Nieuwenhuizen, with whom I travelled around Scotland three times during the 1990s. Part of our adventures can be read in *The Road to Craigellachie Revisited*. The second one is Marcel van Gils, aka Mr Laphroaig Collector, possessing an impressive number of bottles containing that iconic brand. We are both members of the Friends of Craigellachie Malt Whisky Club and met each other in the hotel for the first time, way back when.

It must have been in 2004, during the Spirit of Speyside festival. Dutch whisky aficionados and collectors Sicco Maathuis and Jeroen Koetsier were present as well. It was one of those legendary whisky evenings, never to be forgotten. At first we enjoyed a whisky dinner with my mentor and comrade in drams, the legendary Michael Jackson. After dinner drams were served in the library, where Jeroen, Full Proof for the cognoscenti, opened a couple of very special bottles, even managing to surprise Michael.

Jeroen not only collects whisky but also whisky books and is an esteemed member of the Craig Club as well. He smartly succeeded in getting Marcel and me to do some labour for him. That evening in the library he told us he wanted to drive to Edinburgh the next day, to value a collection for a gentleman who had inherited a bunch of bottles from his father. The son was not interested in whisky and decided to sell the lot. And indeed, the following morning Jeroen drove southwards, whereas Marcel and I went to nearby Dufftown to enjoy ourselves visiting a couple of distilleries.

In the evening Jeroen returned to the Craig, openly excited. He pulled up a chair in the Quaich bar, threw his exhausted frame in it and looked us straight in the eye. 'My car is filled to the roof with bottles. Some very precious ones among them.' With a satisfied look on his face he ordered a dram, suddenly frowning. 'Darn, I have a rental car, because I took the plane to come here. But you two are with the ferry and your own cars, aren't you?' he wickedly smiled. 'So, you may be able to take the bottles to The Netherlands for me.' He didn't even ask, he more or less stated it as a fact.

Marcel and I looked at each other and couldn't help bursting out in laughter. 'Hey, that thought didn't cross your mind earlier today, did it?' I replied. With something that might have been a guilty expression, were it not for his smiling eyes, he answered: 'Well, eh, I didn't immediately think about it.'

Never kick a man when he is down, so I instantly offered to take part of the collection in my car. I was travelling alone and had ample space, but not enough for all the bottles. At the time I drove a BMW Z3 which is a nice car, but with the disadvantage that the concept 'boot' is not overdeveloped in that type of vehicle. Marcel had to convince his wife. At first she found it a bit nerve-wrecking to cross the North Sea and two country borders with so many bottles, but Marcel found a way to soothe her mind. We both had one caveat. If Customs and Excise Officers wanted to take anything or fine us, it would be Jeroen's responsibility. Happy as a clam he helped us a few days later to fill up our cars and I left for Roseisle near Edinburgh, to take the ferry to Zeebrugge in Belgium. At the time that ferry still transported passengers as well as trucks. I doubt that ever after any other two-seater would ride the Scottish roads with so many bottles of whisky aboard.

On the Scottish side no questions were asked and I could drive the Z3 safely on board, locking it securely and covering my precious load with a few tartan blankets. The next morning the ferry moored in Zeebrugge and I felt rather nervous. With my heart racing I drove up to the Customs office. 'Nothing to declare?' 'No, sir, nothing!' The bottles were packaged in anonymous carton boxes without any print on them, still covered by the throws.

Approximately four hours later I parked the car in front of my house in Zwolle and started to unload the car. Hardly had I finished when the telephone rang. 'Hey, it's Jeroen, did all my bottles make it undamaged?' he asked without a trace of empathy for the concerned driver. 'Yes, and so did I', I sighed. 'Well, I will come and collect them first thing tomorrow.' Jeroen only lives a good 45 minutes away. And indeed, at nine sharp the following morning the doorbell rang. We moved the bottles from the hallway into Jeroen's car. When he parted he gave me a small bottle of Kinclaith, an extremely rare single malt, with which I have a special connection. A connection Jeroen knew of. We would not see each other for many years after that event – until we ran into each other at Maltstock.

Not so with Marcel. We'd enjoyed each other's company in Scotland and he also succeeded in transporting Jeroen's 'contraband' safely to The Netherlands. So, we had an adventure in common. Back in The Netherlands we kept in touch and after a while Marcel invited Becky and I to come and visit. He wanted to show us his collection of Laphroaig bottles. It turned out to be another memorable evening.

Marcel namely had a plan and introduced it as follows: 'I am a dentist with a collection, happily married with Leonoor, we deliberately chose not to start a family, apart from owning a little dog. I want to leave something behind and you can write. Do you want to write a book about my collection?'

Ah, Mr van Gils looked for immortality on the bookshelf. Well, that's something we can deliver. But, to just focus on the bottles seemed a bit boring to me. So I suggested turning it into a historical publication about Laphroaig distillery, written around his stunning collection. During the evening our enthusiasm for the project grew. For me especially when Marcel mentioned he would finance the entire venture and hire us to make the book. A writer's dream, since I usually have to invest much time, money and energy in writing a book and it can take a few years to see the first sincere amount of royalties flowing into my bank account.

It did not take long after that evening for us to decide to make *The Legend of Laphroaig*. As a threesome, since Becky was of indispensible assistance during the project that ran for 15 consecutive months in 2006 and 2007. We requested and were granted exclusive access to Laphroaig's archives by brand owner Beam Global. The archives were partly stored at the distillery, partly at Glasgow University's Library.

On Friday 9 November 2007, at the opening of the International Whisky Festival in Leiden, the official launch of the book was celebrated. Charles Maclean held a brief talk and handed the first copy to long time distillery manager Iain Henderson, nicknamed Mr Laphroaig and co-creator of the Friends of Laphroaig loyalty program. Master blender Robert Hicks also joined the party. Those whisky enthusiasts who wanted to purchase a copy that day, could do so at the whisky books stand of Sanne and Sebastian Smits, who specialise in drinks books, ever-present at the festival. Charlie, Iain, Robert, Marcel and I signed many copies that evening and the stocks ran extremely low. Beam Global thanked us with a special very limited version of Laphroaig – a 27-year-old matured in sherry casks.

At such a moment you forget the hard labour of the past one-and-a-half years. Labour that lead to one of my favourite whisky books to date. Without Marcel it might not have come into existence, since he played a crucial role in the project. Not only as collector and financier. Marcel is, just like Becky and I, fond of research and we could really have a go at it for *The Legend.* Whereas I had conceived the format and written a first draft and outline, Marcel prepared our research trip. When the three of us we took off for Glasgow and entered the university library, he had already arranged a whole list of documents we'd probably want to study. The man in charge of the archives had images, letters and such organised and coded on a large table in the room we were to occupy during the coming week. Whatever we needed to be digitised we put to the left. When only photocopies were required, the originals were put to the right.

Eventually Becky found an old letter, dated 1835/1836, in a forgotten old box. It was a correspondence between Laphroaig's founding brothers Donald and Alexander Johnston, dealing with the sales of the latter's shares to the former. I still remember her saying in her usual modest manner: 'Guys, I think I found something very interesting.' That evening we celebrated Becky 's unique find with dinner at the Ubiquitous Chip in the trendy West end neighbourhood of Glasgow.

Research on the isle of Islay was a feast in itself. How often in life are you presented with the opportunity to be present at a distillery for five days and nights, whenever it suits you to come or leave? To make photographs wherever you wish? Interview whom you want? Open old cupboards, book cases at will? Or spend hours in the warehouses surrounding the distillery?

Talks with the stillman on duty at midnight, listening to his stories that would end up as anecdotes in the book to come. An afternoon at the maltings, putting peat on the fire with your own hands. Assisting with mashing and fermentation. Being in the way regularly without noticing it. But also, enjoying a midnight dram under the moonlight at an almost deserted distillery. We did it all, with gusto, and respect.

Laphroaig didn't have a coffee shop or restaurant so during lunch hours we would leave for Ardbeg and enjoy a quick meal in the former Kilns with Jackie Thomson. After all it's just around the corner from Laphroaig.

Evenings and nights were spent in Port Ellen at the Oyster Catcher B&B, at the time owned by Lynn Ross. (A few years later she would sell the place and leave the island). Lynn would grow into a saviour for Marcel one day. It was during the weekend. It being Easter, Becky and I wanted to go to a little church near Bridgend. Marcel decided to spend some time at Port Ellen's burial ground in order to take photographs of the Johnstons interred there. Then he would walk to the water source of Laphroaig to photograph the Kilbride dam. In the early afternoon we would meet at Machir Bay, on the Atlantic side of Islay to jointly take an afternoon walk.

We waited for half an hour, an hour – no signal on the GSM – two hours, and finally, Marcel's car appeared in the distance. A tad downtrodden he got out of his car and apologised for the delay. 'But I really could not help it, honestly!' And then he told us what had happened. Having succeeded in his mission at the graveyard he'd tried to rapidly cross some fields in order to get as close to the water source as possible. Halfway he tripped over a barbed wire fence and fell into a stinky brown mess. 'A decomposed dead sheep', he sighed disgustedly. Smelling rotten, feeling utterly uncomfortable, he found his way back to the Oyster Catcher where Lynn took his soiled trousers, put them in the washing machine and poured him a stiff dram. 'You could have taken the car, there is a broad road to the dam and it will only take you five minutes', she tried to encourage him. After having changed his clothes, Marcel then hit the road, arriving much later than planned at Machir Bay.

We decided to drive to Finlaggan, to see the old ruins of the castle where the Lords of the Isles used to meet, centuries ago. The wind was menacingly cold and Marcel still hadn't entirely recovered from his encounter with a dead animal. Hence I took care of the photos that afternoon. I do part-time photography and sell images to other publishers, but would not consider myself a fulltime pro. Marcel is an excellent photographer and although not officially trained, in my eyes he's better than many a professional. In fact, I consider him to be one. In later years he would supply photography for a series of my other publications, among others four small books on champagne and on golf.

It illustrates that, after having completed our project, we really wanted to continue to work together if an occasion should occur. Writing a book like *The Legend of Laphroaig* is not an easy one, whether you do it alone, or you are assisted by others in photography, research and editing. Working with Marcel was an interesting challenge. From the start he was focused on detail, whereas I am working along broad lines as long as I am conceiving a manuscript. I won't write whole chapters immediately. This difference in approach regularly led to misunderstandings and minor clashes between the two of us.

Upon our return from Glasgow and Islay we had a wealth of material to choose from and Marcel, as the one who assigned the project to us, demanded a complete draft of a chapter within weeks. That's not the way I work, I need ample time to get it right in my thoughts before I trust a letter or paragraph to paper, or hard disk if you prefer, apart from an outline and notes that only I can understand in that phase of a manuscript. It took a while before Marcel understood that. On the other hand I had to get used to the fact that he, as a dentist, was used to work on tiny details day-in-day-out,

often seeing the end result the same day.

In that early phase of getting to know and understand each other better, Becky was an important buffer who had empathy for both our arguments, as different as they may have been sometimes. When discussions tended to get too hot, she knew perfectly how to cool us down again.

When I finally emailed Marcel the first chapter – still in concept phase – the next hurdle had to be taken. He sent it back with the following remark: 'Hey Frodo, this isn't *The Lord of the Rings*!' That facts need a bit of fiction as cement between the bricks and that fiction for similar reasons may be part of the foundation of certain facts, took time to sink in with the always very motivated dentist/part-time photographer/researcher. But let it be well understood: *The Legend* is as historically accurate as we were able to make it with the material we rendered from the archives at the time.

When the book was written and published Becky and I considered our task done. Marcel however continued to do extra research and discovered a few places of incompleteness. He also managed to track down descendants of Alexander Johnston in Australia and still keeps in touch with them.

And that's where Laphroaig's story continued for him for a while, whereas we were done with it and already prepared for another book. *The Legend* sold out a few years ago and Marcel wasn't interested in doing a new print run. End of story, at least that was what we thought. People still asked for a copy and we had to disappoint them. Sometimes a copy was offered online against hugely inflated prices, which had never been our intention.

***

One night in 2014 I could not sleep and poured myself a dram of Laphroaig and looked at the bottle. Suddenly I realised that the following year would be Laphroaig's bicentenary. I scribbled down some thoughts on the note pad I always keep at my bedside table. The next morning I reread them and they still made sense. At our morning work meeting, which we usually do during breakfast, I told Becky: 'I have a cunning plan. Why shouldn't we approach Laphroaig and ask them to do a new book for their 200th anniversary?' Becky is always critical but supportive about new ideas – I usually come up with 20 or more a week – and asked: 'How do you see that?'

Now she got me talking. 'I won't concentrate it on a collection as with *The Legend*, but focus on the people who make it and the people who enjoy it. I also want to write more about the different phases in the actual production process at the distillery, interview employees and revisit the archives. And of course I will ask Marcel to join the project.' Becky gave it her blessing. Marcel, when approached, wasn't too enthusiastic about it. He was of the opinion that Laphroaig wouldn't be interested, but would like to be involved should a new book be made after all.

I pitched the idea to Laphroaig's distillery manager John Campbell and he immediately liked it. Within weeks we received a positive answer. Beam Suntory UK was seriously interested in the project. A few days later I phoned Marcel to get him on board for additional research, photography and editorial skills. This time however we would finance the project ourselves and hire him as a paid contributor. The roles reversed as it were, compared to 2007. For the record, we wanted to write and publish a sequel with his invaluable assistance.

To cut an already long story short, we published *1815-2015 – 200 Years of Laphroaig* in November 2015. It's entirely different from *The Legend*, albeit that part of the history of the distillery was taken from it, amended, augmented and re-written by me, where needed, with the ever critical eyes of Becky and Marcel, to correct my errors. Beam Global decided to buy all stock from our publishing company Conceptual Continuity and uses the book partly for promotional purposes, partly as merchandise on Laphroaig's website; whiskyboeken.nl holds a retail license. Hence, this book can't be purchased in regular bookstores. End of story this time. I don't think I have a third book about Laphroaig in me.

Campbeltown Loch

Campbeltown Loch,
I wish ye were whisky,
Aye, I wish ye were whisky,
I would drink ye dry

This song, made famous by artist Andy Stewart, brings to mind days gone by, when this part of Scotland was famous for its many distilleries and the city of Campbeltown considered the epicentre of malt whisky.

This small town, on the tip of the Kintyre peninsula, has witnessed rocky times but shown to be a sturdy survivor through the ages. In the 17th and 18th century the name was almost eponymous with smuggling, the coastline with its many coves an excellent hiding place for the men whose profession was once considered honourable. Whether it was legal or not, that business meant an economic stimulus for this remote part of the Scottish mainland. Times changed after 1823 when a law was passed that made it much easier and cheaper to obtain a license for whisky distilling. Campbeltown flourished and legal distilling operations mushroomed during the following decades, culminating in more than 30 distilleries. By the mid 1800s Campbeltown was known as the 'Whisky Capital of the World' and considered a whisky production region of its own. The small town bustled with life; it also served as a main port to Ireland and the Western Isles. But times changed again and this time not for the better. By the turn of the 19th century, the whisky industry at large suffered a severe collapse, caused by the so-called Pattison crash in 1898. A large company led by the Pattison brothers not only tampered with the quality of the whisky but also with the accounting. The brothers went to trial and were sentenced to prison, but the whisky industry was punished, too. For a time Scotch whisky had a bad reputation and Campbeltown in particular was hit hard. Combined with the coming of other means of transportation, most notably the railways, the port and all its immediate activities went into a steep decline. The post-war depression in the late 1920s and early 1930s plus Prohibition in the United States did the rest. In 1934 the distilleries of Glen Scotia and Springbank were the only ones producing whisky. It would take 70 years before a third distillery joined their ranks.

Glen Scotia was founded in 1832 by the Gailbraith family and can be considered a real stop-and-go concern. Taken over many times, mothballed during several longer periods of time, neglected, run by staff of another distillery, closed, reopened, and for sale, as we heard through the grape-vine, or should we say grain-vine? However the maturing stocks are not part of the deal. That makes it difficult to find an investor, since it would take at least a year to restore Glen Scotia and then another 10 years to mature whisky, without a return on investment for at least a decade. Glen Scotia is not usually open to visitors, but we were allowed to take a look inside. On the one hand it was sad to see such a run-down distillery, but on the other hand it was a good opportunity to see how things were in the past, before (necessary) modernisation and automation took control of many a distillery. Glen Scotia ran at only 15% of its capacity and was operated by two men, one of whom a retiree from the Springbank distillery. The whisky has been released at different ages over the years, first bottled at 8 and 14 years; in 2005 being replaced by a 12-year-old. The 14-year-old can still be found in many a liquor store. Several vintages are available. The blended (aka vatted) malt Glengyle is also produced by today's owner Loch Lomond Distillers, who registered Glengyle as a trademark in 1995. Very recently the distillery has been refurbished and even has a small shop and visitor centre.

The history of the Springbank distillery is well documented and dates back to 1828 when the Reid family founded the distillery, the 14th erected in Campbeltown. Within nine years the Reids ran into financial trouble, regardless of the whisky boom and were offered help by their in-laws the Mitchell family. The latter bought the distillery in 1837 and since then descendants of the Mitchells have inherited the business. In 1897 a William Mitchell risked opening a new distillery called Glengyle. His brother John continued operation at Springbank. William was the less fortunate of the two. Glengyle closed in 1925, only having produced whisky for 28 years. From then on its buildings would be used for storage. Springbank suffered and had to close between 1926 and 1933, but did start up production after that silent period. In 1960 the company closed its malting floors and began to buy malted barley from elsewhere. When the independent bottler Cadenhead came up for sale in 1969, they were added to the Mitchell portfolio. A few years later the distillery began to experiment with a heavily peated variety that ultimately would become known as Longrow. The next decade (1979-1989) Springbank would be closed for the second time in its existence, albeit that the first Longrow bottling was launched during that period, in 1985. From 1987 the production started on a limited base, not to reach full capacity until 1990. Two years after that Springbank decided to reopen its malting floors, making it one of the few distilleries to have the entire production from malting to bottling on-site. In 1997 a third, un-peated, variety was added and named Hazelburn, after an old Campbeltown distillery that had operated between 1796 and 1925 and was once owned by Sir Peter Mackie of Lagavulin fame.

In 2004 a little miracle happened. Glengyle distillery

arose from its ashes and was opened by Mr. Hedley Wright, Springbank's primary owner and a direct descendant of the Mitchells. The whisky made in that neat and tiny distillery, directly behind Springbank, cannot be called by its proper name, since Glen Scotia/Loch Lomond owns the trade name. Hence its whisky is presented under the name Kilkerran. That name can etymologically be traced back to the Kintyre peninsula, whose Gaelic name was Kinlochkilkerran, in English meaning 'the head of the loch by the church of St Kieran.' I'm always amazed by the compactness of the Gaelic language.

Despite the fact that it has only three working distilleries, Campbeltown survived as an independent whisky region. The distinctive tastes of Springbank and Longrow as well as the resurrection of Glengyle surely contribute to that state.

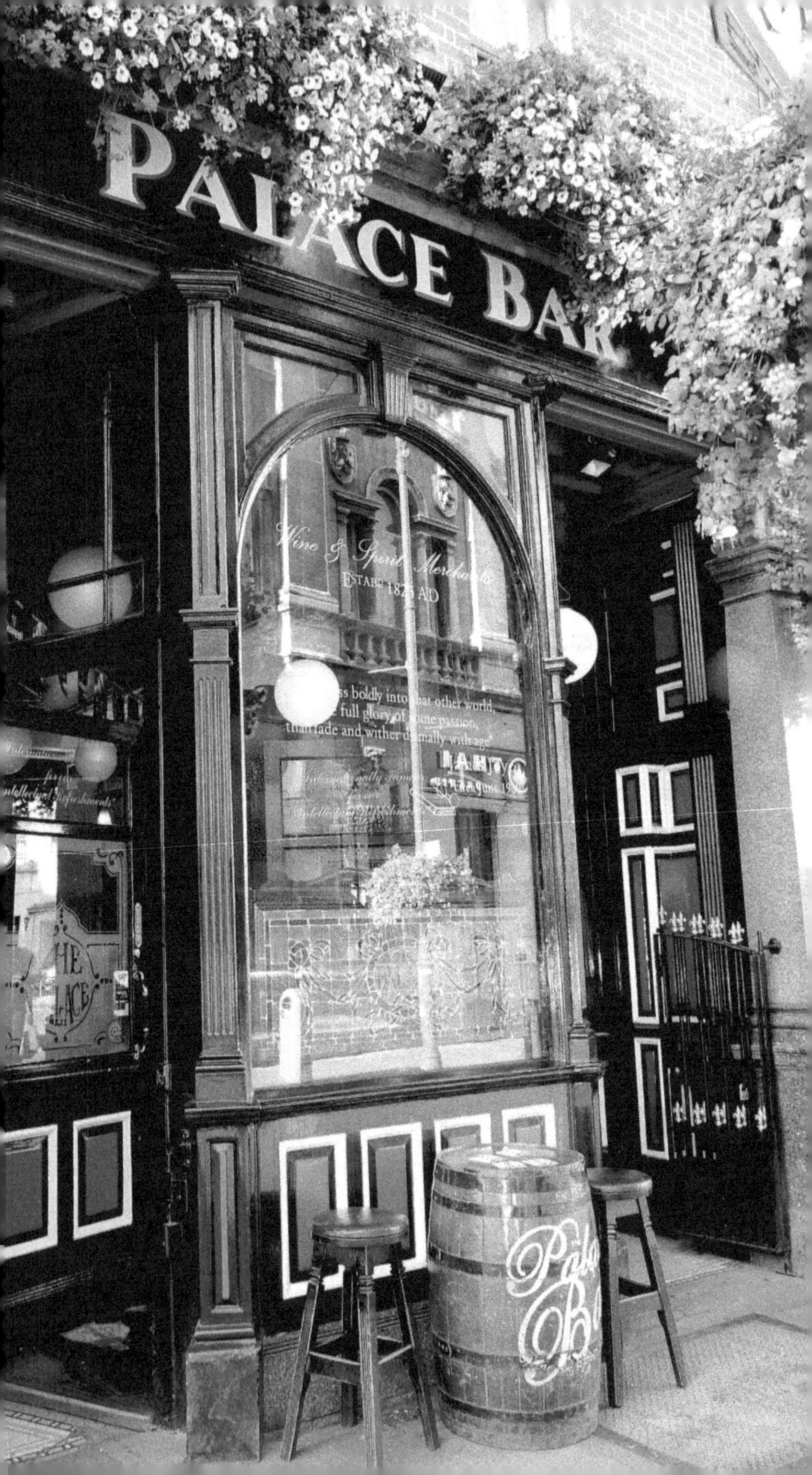
PALACE BAR

Ireland, Here We Come!

Scotland has had one for more than 22 years. It is called the Malt Whisky Trail. The Bourbon Trail was founded in 1999 in the USA. Strangely enough there was no such thing in the cradle of whiskey distilling – Ireland. *Was*, since a remarkable woman named Heidi Donelon saw her brainchild born in 2009.

Heidi is a phenomenon. We met her for the first time in 2008 in Paris, France, during the annual whisky festival. There she unfolded her plans for a true Ireland whiskey trail. She knows what she is talking about, having worked quite a few years for Irish Distillers, the makers of Jameson, Paddy's and Powers, leaving that job to become an independent whiskey consultant. One year later Heidi had convinced more than 30 companies to become part of her idea: the Ireland Whiskey Trail. The Irish whiskey industry is highly concentrated, with (at the time) only three operating distilleries in the republic and one in Northern Ireland. Among them they produce nearly 100 different whiskeys. However, there is much more to see on the trail, as we would soon find.

In December 2009 Heidi approached us with a request, 'Would the Whiskey Couple be interested in travelling the trail and writing articles about it?' It took us a split second to say 'Yes.' Becky and Heidi started planning and in July 2010 we sailed to the Emerald Isle with an itinerary that was crammed to the limit. In 12 days we were supposed to visit 24 pubs, three working distilleries, a few whisky museums, three golf resorts and 12 hotels, restaurants and B&B's. A challenge we couldn't refuse.

When we returned home our car had covered over 4,000 kilometres and we were amazed, taken, fatigued, happy to have been there, sad to have left and on the road we had made many new friends. Each place on the trail we could easily have stayed a week or more, but the tight schedule made that impossible. The beauty of it is that we have reason to return, time and again.

The Ireland Whiskey Trail is so extensive that it is indeed better to cut it into digestible pieces, instead of what we did. Heidi designed the trail in such a way that the interested traveller can choose his own destinations and timeframe. The website www.irelandwhiskeytrail.com offers the opportunity to freely download a map of the entire trail. It is a fine tool to decide where to go and where to spend time and money, and experience the unmatched congeniality of the Irish. In the course of one chapter it is simply impossible to tell the entire story of our trip, so we've spread it out over a few. Now, where to start? Dublin? Cork? Connemara? Sligo? Kilbeggan?

Well, let's give it a go in Ireland's capital. Heidi booked us in the beautiful modern Brooks Hotel, just outside Temple Bar – the famous district of Dublin where the eponymous bar is the centre of attention. This is a must see. The Temple Bar itself offers over 400 different whiskeys and entertains their guests with traditional live music nearly every evening of the week. The exterior as well as the interior is pleasing to the eye. The Palace Bar, on the other end of Temple Bar, is a fine example of an original Victorian pub. In the upstairs room, you are sure to find 'trad' music: traditional Irish music. Will Aherne, third generation to own the place, showed us some very old Jameson bottles that belonged to his grandfather. They decorate the bar, unopened. Adorning the walls of the cosy back room are portraits and photographs of famous Irish writers and journalists. This room was the unofficial office of the spirited Bertie Smylie, editor of *The Irish Times* from 1934 until his death in 1954. A framed drawing shows Bertie riding his bicycle with a typewriter balanced on the handlebars and a bottle of Scotch in his pocket – his father was Scottish, which might explain the choice of whisky.

Although Dublin is the birthplace of Jameson Distillery (1780), no whiskey has been made at that location since 1975, when the entire production was moved to Midleton, County Cork, where a brand new distillery was built. Luckily the old buildings were kept and beautifully restored. They now house a museum, located on Bow Street, where the visitor is taken back more than 250 years to when John Jameson decided to enter the whiskey business. Many old artefacts were kept and are now on display. A tour will take you around the distillery as it would have been in the old days and ends in a tutored tasting of various Jameson expressions. In one of the former warehouses, where the old wooden beams are still supporting the roof, a beautiful shop has been created and the in-house restaurant is well-appreciated by local business people for lunch meetings, as well as by whiskey tourists.

Dublin once was a thriving whiskey capital. With the decline of the business, fuelled by various economical and agricultural disasters, among which the potato famine of the 1850s and Prohibition in the first part of the 20th century, the leading role that Ireland possessed with its whiskeys dwindled. As a consequence distilling became a highly concentrated activity, with only a handful of owners pulling the ropes. Nowadays Irish Distillers – a subsidiary of Pernod Ricard – not only produces Jameson, currently the best selling Irish whiskey worldwide, but also the famous Redbreast and Powers. The former is a pure pot still whiskey and the latter a blend. The impressive remains of Powers' pot stills can be seen in the courtyard of the National College of Art and Design that now inhabits those old distillery buildings. One of the steam engines is still mostly intact, but its room is sadly used as a storage facility.

Dublin city also harbours the only specialist whisk(e)y retailer in the republic – The Celtic Whisky Shop. It is run by Ally Alpine, a Scotsman. In the two weeks that followed we heard his name over and over, since he also supplies many pubs throughout Ireland. You may find a bottle of 12-year-old Green Spot whiskey here; these were bottled by Dublin wine merchants Mitchell & Son, owners of the only brand produced for and sold by an independent wine merchant in Ireland. In former days it was common for wine merchants to blend and produce their own whiskey brands. More likely you will find their smooth 10-year-old Green Spot, also a pure pot still Irish whiskey, meaning the whiskey is distilled only in copper pot stills, not in a column still. Our second evening in Dublin we enjoyed a very tasty dinner in Brooks and the bartender poured us a delicious dram of Celtic Nations. To our knowledge it is the only blend of Irish and Scottish whisk(e)y in the world. It shows again how well these two can go together. After all, the Irish Scoti tribe invaded Alba and named it Scotland way back when.

Only two days in Ireland – 1 hotel, 1 whiskey museum, 1 former distillery and 2 pubs down. 20-something to go! We'll be back on the Ireland Whiskey Trail in the coming chapters, entertaining you with more stories about this amazing part of the (whiskey) world.

Fast forward to 2016: Since our visit in 2010, I've been back a couple of times, the main reason for visits being a new wave of craft distilleries throughout the country. Dublin can now boast Teeling Distillery and Tullamore has its own distillery back, brand new, built by current owner WM Grant & Sons of Glenfiddich fame. In total more than 10 distilleries joined the ranks, with many more in the works, both in the Irish Republic and in Northern Ireland.

Scotsmen in Ireland

A visit to Jameson Heritage Centre is an excellent introduction to the history of Irish whiskey. Jameson is by far the bestselling Irish whiskey in the world. Although this whiskey has been made in the southern part of Ireland since 1971, it all started more to the north, in Dublin, in the last quarter of the 18th century.

John Jameson wasn't born in Ireland but rather in Scotland in 1749. He moved to Dublin in 1770, aged 21, at the time the epicentre of whiskey, quality whiskey that is. Being a complete outsider to the trade didn't discourage him in the least. On the contrary – in the 16th century his ancestors were awarded for their courage in fighting the pirates on the world seas. Their motto *Sine metu* became his inspiration, meaning 'without fear'. With such a guideline you can conquer a world. He bought an existing distillery at Bow Street and turned it towards his life's goal: to make the best Irish whiskey in the world. Thus he became a true Irishman – not by birth, but by distillation.

John Jameson was obsessed with quality and was personally involved in selecting the right type of barley and the best casks he could get hold of. He accepted the fact that quality comes at a price and was loved by his suppliers. His colleague distillers weren't so enthusiastic and considered his approach as an unnecessary attempt to drive up purchase prices of raw materials and whiskey. At the time double distillation was the norm, in Scotland as well as in Ireland. Jameson started to experiment with multiple distillation (three, four, even five times). According to him triple distillation delivered the true product – smooth, tasty and subtle. Whether he became the trendsetter for this type of distilling method is not known.

In 1887 the famous whisky chronicler Alfred Barnard noted, after a visit to Jameson in Dublin: 'The Bow Street Distillery, which is one of the oldest in Ireland, having been established about the year 1780, covers upwards of five acres of ground, and is a quarter of a mile from the Four Courts, and about half a mile from Sackville Street, credited with being the broadest street in Europe. The water used in the Distillery is obtained from two deep wells on the premises, noted from time immemorial for its quality, purity and suitability for distillation purposes.' In short, a distinguished location to create whiskey.

In the 200 years to come it was always a descendant of John Jameson managing the company. This ended in 1988 when Pernod Ricard acquired the distillery. But let's not run ahead of the Jameson's family history. Around 1891 sales figures of Jameson started to drop. This marked the beginning of a decline. In the following decades the prominent place of Irish whiskey on the world market was taken over by Scotch whisky and 'Irish' turned into a mere shadow of its former glory. In 1902 venture capitalists were willing to invest and turned John Jameson & Sons into a public company. John Jameson IV's place was taken by Andrew Jameson who succeeded in steering the company to a safe harbour, even during Prohibition, which wreaked havoc in the Irish whiskey industry as a whole. In the 1960s Jameson returned to its former splendour. An important step was the management's decision to stop outsourcing the bottling of the product to independent brokers, but creating in-house facilities instead. From then on Jameson no longer delivered in bulk to third parties.

1971 witnessed the decision to close Bow Street Distillery, grown to more than four acres, and move the production of Jameson and other brands made-to-order, like Powers, Tullamore Dew, Redbreast and Paddy, to Midleton, near Cork in the southern part of Ireland. In 1988 the company was acquired by the French and is still owned by Pernod Ricard's subsidiary Irish Distillers. The buildings in Dublin were left abandoned and dilapidated at a steady pace. Luckily they were saved for posterity in 2007, when the complex was restored with a budget of five million Euros. The result is the Jameson Heritage Centre.

***

It's Tuesday and we take an early start, driving to Cahir in County Tipperary, in order to visit Malone's Galtee Inn. Again a fine example of a Victorian pub with wooden panelling throughout. Owner John prepares a 'hot Irish' – hot water, Irish whiskey, and a slice of lemon with whole cloves stuck into it. It is one of his specialties. He is very proud of his collection of old Irish whiskeys – a collection he quietly assembled over the course of many years.

On we go, to Midleton, County Cork, for a lunch appointment at the Jameson Experience Midleton. This whiskey museum is housed in the old Cork Distillery, which produced whiskey for more than 150 years before it was closed. Irish Distillers has concentrated the making of all its brands here in a modern distillery situated behind the old buildings, not accessible to visitors. Although the audiovisual is the same as the one we saw in Dublin, save the first 30 seconds, the museum certainly is not a copy of the other. The Irish may have been a tad late with establishing their own whiskey trail, but they saved their heritage in a way that can be an example to many a Scottish distillery.

We spend the evening and night in the Castlemartyr Resort, a five star hotel 10 minutes from Midleton Distillery. The old estate has been converted into a beautiful 18 hole golf course and in the manor we enter the impressive

Knight's Bar, sporting a fine whiskey selection. It's 2010 and World Cup Football is on our minds. In the clubhouse at the golf course we watch and see the Dutch team beat Uruguay and the 'orange team' reaches the finals for the third time in its existence. Will they finally become the champion this year?

Pub Crawl

The next day we hit the road again at an early hour and steer our car direction Crosshaven to interview the owner of Cronin's pub. Sean Cronin is a true connoisseur of the Irish water of life and presents a fabulous tasting with very old Midletons. When asked what people do for a living in this distant nook of the country, he smiles: 'Crosshaven is a drinking town with a fishing problem.'

After a delicious lunch consisting of fried crab claws in garlic butter we have to leave, much to our regret, since we could have talked with Sean for many hours. We head for the Tap Tavern in the historic town of Kinsale where we meet the 80-something publican Mary and her son Brian, who conducts ghost tours in this tourist town with the many coloured houses. The Tap Tavern is one of the few pubs left in Ireland where time stood still. It seems that nothing has changed in over 100 years. Some very old bottles of whiskey behind the bar carry a label 'not for sale'.

And further we travel, to Douglas – a suburb of Cork – for a meeting with the O'Connor brothers. After a stint in the USA they came back to their home country to continue the family business, the South County Bar. This is a large pub with a special Irish Whiskey Corner. We spend evening and night in the Hayfield Manor Hotel, home to a well-stocked whiskey bar. Its manager Claire O'Donohue is expecting us and presents us with a liquid surprise. Life is hard. The hotel is situated in the middle of the city of Cork, but that is hardly noticeable. Of all the places we stayed during the entire Irish trip this turned out to be our favourite one.

Thursday morning at 8 am sharp, with the car all loaded up, we aim for Bandon, to try and find the ruins of the Allman distillery. Nowadays the majority of the Irish whiskey industry is concentrated in the hands of a few, but in previous times that was not the case. Travellers with a sharp eye for detail may discover many old distilleries, or what is left of them. So with Allman's, one of the remaining warehouses is converted in an agrarian hardware store that also sells cattle feed. Allman's history is a story in itself for another day. What was once the distillery manager's office now houses a pub – The Old Still Bar. We knock on the door. No answer. The opening hours of the pub are extremely irregular and unpredictable.

There is some serious scenic photography to do and we take the car to the Beara peninsula, below the Ring of Kerry, described by locals as more beautiful than the Ring so praised by many tourists. The weather is not our friend this afternoon, so the harvest is meagre. We try a tiny bit of the Ring, but take the weather with us. We are cold and wet by now and more than happy to check in at the Killarney Park Hotel. Food & Beverage Manager Eion Traynor awaits us in the Garden Bar with a tasting. We slowly discover what Heidi Donelon has done in the past years. She not only assembled the Ireland Whiskey Trail, but also trained staff of many pubs, restaurants and hotels. They all speak very highly of her, as does Eion.

After the tasting a taxi collects us and brings us in 15 minutes to the Beaufort Bar, owned by Padruig O'Sullivan, a man who needs to be interviewed. Padruig is a proponent of the 'Open Bottle Philosophy' and we are offered Irish whiskeys we've never heard of before and which brands seldom if never appear on the shelves of liquor stores and bars. Meanwhile Padruig entertains us with his vast knowledge of the Irish whiskey history. In the dead of night the cab driver brings us back to the hotel, safe and sound...

***

My iPhone shows me that it is Friday 9 July. Heidi has been very compassionate with us. We can finally sleep in. We are only expected in the Creamery Bar in Bunratty about lunchtime. This building is one of the original stopping places of the Bianconi Coach Service, a company that arranged stagecoach routes throughout Ireland in the 19th century. Around 1927 this particular station was converted into a tiny dairy factory. Just a few years ago, its third lease of life presented itself in the form of a genuine pub. Noel, one of the owners, explains about the whiskey preferences of the average customers. For years Paddy's or Powers was the beverage of choice, but recently Jameson has won them over. It won't matter to Pernod-Ricard, since the French drinks company owns all three brands. Before we leave, Noel serves us the house specialty – bread pudding with whiskey.

Unfortunately our busy itinerary does not leave room to visit Bunratty Castle opposite the Creamery. We are supposed to drive to the Burren now. The weather still isn't ideal, but we manage to immortalise this unique piece of earth with our cameras. It is so barren, so desolate, but at the same time utterly intriguing. Centuries ago those Irish that, according to Cromwell (1599-1658) did not belong to Irish society anymore, were banned to this horrendous region where nothing grows. Many a desperate Irishman chose to escape this fate and left from the Burren to America, hoping to find a better life across the Atlantic Ocean.

This is the region of Connaught. Its barrenness may have been best described by one of Cromwell's officers, Edmund Ludlow: '(Burren) is a country where there is not enough water to drown a man, nor wood enough to hang one, nor earth enough to bury him.' Nevertheless, the views are impressive. Between rain showers we shoot beautiful pictures. Slowly the weather changes for the better, but that won't do us any good. We have to continue our journey, with more pubs on the travel schedule. The first one we encounter after our brief stint at the Burren is O'Donohue's in Fanore, on the west coast. The young publican named Pat is the third generation owner. The building can be seen from afar, brightly painted blue as it is, you cannot miss it. Pat is a real whisky aficionado and certainly not one-track, or one-dram minded. Until now we experienced a true domination of the Irish cratur in the pubs and restaurants we visited. Pat however has a broader mind and is building up a tremendous, international collection. His Scottish whiskies come from, have a guess, yes, Ally Alpine from the Celtic Whisky Shop in Dublin.

At dusk we arrive in Ballyvaughn and check into our B&B – the eponymous Lodge. Heidi's preparations for our quest were thorough. The places where she has us stay are a proper mix of five star hotels, small family inns and B&Bs. We get a fine impression of what the country has to offer. Wherever we show up, the Irish we meet are cordial and friendly, without any airs. We really feel welcome, time and again.

A few hundred meters from the B&B is O'Lochlainn's Irish Whiskey Pub – definitely one of the highlights of the trip as we would soon experience. Owners are the couple Peter and Margareth. They do not open before 9 pm, which is highly unusual for an Irish pub. There are two reasons why. Margareth is a cooking teacher and daily has to travel three hours back and forth to her school. Peter is a farmer and owns milking cows as well as meat cows. It is a sheer miracle that the twosome manages to run a cosy and well-visited pub in the hours in-between. Margareth is everything you wish an Irish landlady to be: funny, friendly, buxom and cordial, with a wicked sense of humour. She shows us the treasure of O'Lochlainn's – an incredible and unique collection of old and very old Scotch and Irish whisk(e)ys, once started by Peter's father. We can take as many images as we like. Margareth cannot reach the top shelf and invites me behind the bar to fetch them myself. I ask her if she wants me to sop the shelves, which causes a raucous laughter among all customers watching what is happening. It's getting late that evening, very late...

Next Saturday morning a meeting with Eamon Howley is planned. Until now he is one of the very few in Ireland who offers tailor-made group travels along the Whiskey Trail. We are supposed to meet at Freeney's Pub & Fishing Tackle Shop. It doubles as a liquor store and has been located in Galway's High Street since who knows how long. Eamon is accompanied by his good friend Willie Henry, a local historian with a series of books to his credit. They extensively inform us about Galway and its attractive medieval city centre. We offer both gentlemen a lunch but they insist on paying for us. No negotiations allowed.

We seal eternal friendship over a pint of Guinness and then leave for the rough and wild lands of Connemara, dotted with many lakes, or loughs as the Irish call them. At the western tip we park the car in front of Lowry's pub in the town of Clifden to examine a collection of whiskeys once assembled by a retired Irish police officer. Sitting at the bar, enjoying a glass, we are entertained by barman Donal O'Brien who at the same time watches a hurling match on telly. He confides that it is a very important game and tries to make us familiar with the rules. This a pure Irish sport, somewhat resembling a mix of football, rugby and field hockey, not unlike Scottish shinty, and is supposedly one of the fastest sports in the world: within a span of four seconds both teams can score a goal.

To get back east we chose a different road and stay the night in Clonbur, in the family owned Fairhill House Hotel. Owner Eddie Lynch employs a Scottish bar manager. His collection shows. We notice a whole series of Gordon & MacPhail's Connoisseurs Choice, among which a genuine

Craigellache single malt! The weather this day had been very rainy again so we could not really make good scenery shots. Instead we try some nice drams before we are served an excellent dinner, something for which the hotel is famous. Eddie is the archetypical, hospitable and welcoming host and does everything in his book to make us feel comfortable. In the evening we enjoy some live trad music. Tired but satisfied, with a belly full, we hit the sack.

***

It's been a week since we arrived in Ireland. When we get up the sun is shining bright with hardly a cloud in sight. The weather is as unpredictable as in Scotland. Eddie takes us on the roof of the hotel where we can admire the panoramas of Connemara. We decide on the spot to first return to the peninsula for some scenic photography before we head north. There is plenty of time, we are not expected in Ballina before 12:30 pm, a mere one-and-a-half hour by car from here. In a good three hours we capture the best of the breathtaking nature that Connemara has to offer and arrive in time at Paddy Jordan's pub. A phenomenon not to go unseen. The word 'cosy' does not enough justice to this place. The ceiling is adorned with old radio parts – Peter, Paddy's son's eccentricity. The food is excellent and so well-appreciated that Peter and his Indian chef won the Gastro Pub Award. The whisky bar is well-stocked and one of the house specialties is Irish salmon marinated in whiskey.

In the afternoon we drive to Enniscrone, some 20 minutes further on up the road, to experience a seaweed bath in Kilcullen. Heidi strongly recommended we take time for this. Since it opened in 1922 this Edwardian bathhouse has not changed a bit. We are offered the 'duo bath room' and within ten minutes we are both lying in two parallel gigantic porcelain bath tubs, immersed in fresh seaweed, collected from the beach that same morning. Instructions on the wall inform us that, when finished, we are expected to scoop the seaweed out of the tubs with our bare hands and deposit it in a bucket. Only much later we would learn that it is offered to farmers, to fertilise the barley fields. So, within a number of years, tiny, tiny particles of Whisky Couple impregnated seaweed may end up in a smooth Irish whiskey, who knows?

At leisure we continue our journey until we reach the Tree Tops B&B in Sligo. We feel utterly relaxed due to the treatment earlier that day and succeed in finding a pub to watch the World Cup Finale. It doesn't end in the best outcome for The Netherlands. On top of that we have the 'luck' that the Irish to the left of our table put all their money on the Dutch team and to our right several Spanish guys cant stop shouting for joy. We managed to curtly congratulate them and sped to our B&B directly after the end signal of the arbiter. It was the only moment during our entire Irish quest that the Irish were less than friendly with us, but only for a moment. That night I dreamt the finale had to be played again and the Dutch beat the Spaniards with 3-0, resulting in us drinking a pint of Guinness with a nip until the early morning. Alas, it was a dream.

Distilling Whisky on a Peninsula

The next morning we are relieved not to be in The Netherlands, after the match the evening before. A three-hour drive brings us to Carlingford on the Cooley peninsula. They distil whiskey here, but not that long.

The year 1987 marked the end of a serious monopoly in the Irish whiskey industry. For decades Irish Distillers had dominated this part of the whiskey market. The one who broke this monopoly was an Irish businessman named John Teeling. However, he had to dig deep before he turned Cooley into a success story 25 years later.

During his university years in the 1970s in Cambridge, Massachusetts, Teeling got the idea of creating some rumour around the Irish whiskey brands. A research project investigating why Irish whiskey as a category had gone into a serious decline fuelled his interest. 17 years later he put idea into practice when he purchased an existing distillery on the Cooley peninsula in the Republic of Ireland. The buildings were erected by Krupps in 1937. This German construction company built three similar plants in Ballina and Dublin. All four distilleries were primarily used for the production of industrial alcohol from rotten potatoes. When the potato disease was overcome, these factories switched to processing molasses into spirit, which was made for Smirnoff vodka in Dublin until 1985. One of the old columns stills used for that purpose stands proudly next to his brothers who now distil spirit for whiskey.

When Teeling acquired the distillery, he teamed up with two old hands who had been working at the plant for decades. One of them is Eddie The Warehouseman, who entertained us for hours and from whom we learnt a lot during our two-day stay at Cooley. Eddie started his career in the drinks industry when he went to work for a company that bought and sold wine and liquor. He explained to us that Cooley makes single grain, blended and single malt whiskeys. He showed us the still houses and we admired three large column stills next to one another. A small gate in the wall leads to a section sporting two gleaming pot stills. Grain and malt whiskey are literally distilled next to each other at Cooley. The grain whiskey is mainly made from corn imported from France. Most of the barley comes from Scotland.

At the plant we see four grain silos, two for corn, one for malted and one for unmalted barley. The latter is needed for Cooley's pure pot still whiskey, traditionally a mix of malted and unmalted barley. The wash backs, or fermentation vessels if you prefer, are separated, too – four for the corn mash and four for the barley mash. They are operated in batches. One column still is made of copper, the others of stainless steel. Both pot stills came from the long closed Watt's distillery in Derry (Northern Ireland). They are the same size and can hold 16,000 litre each. Let's dwell on Watt's for a bit longer.

In 1839 David Watt purchased the Abbey Street Distillery in Derry, which would grow into the largest distillery in the whole of Ireland by 1887, due to next generation Andrew Watt. At the time an incredible two million imperial gallons were produced annually (about 9 million litres). In comparison, Glenfiddich would produce about 10 million litres annually one century later (its output has grown since to about 14 million).

Watt's primary brands were Tyrconnell, Inishowen and Favourite. The first one was named after a racehorse with which the Watts had won a fortune at the National Produce Stakes in 1876. The horse, a complete outsider, won with 100:1 odds. Before Prohibition hit the USA, Tyrconnell was one of the best selling whiskeys in the country, even advertising on billboards in the New York Yankees stadium. The brand enjoyed success in England, Canada, Australia and Nigeria, too. Due to a series of unfortunate historical events in the early 20th century (as can be read elsewhere in this book), the Irish whiskey industry would collapse and with it Watt's, which closed its doors in 1925, taking down the Tyrconnell brand in its wake.

Andrew Watt died three years later in England. Watt's was not resurrected, but Tyrconnell was. The brand name was owned by one of John Teeling's business partners who co-invested in the distillery. They decided to give the revered whiskey brand a second life. Today it is a very agreeable, light, unpeated single malt we love to drink in Spring.

Together with Greenore (single grain), Kilbeggan (blend) and Connemara (peated single malt), Tyrconnell formed the core range of Cooley. At least during the time we visited the distillery. In 2015 Greenore was decommissioned and a new single grain brand launched, confusedly named Kilbeggan, too.

The man responsible for the many whiskeys that leave Cooley is Noel Sweeny, already employed at the site when industrial alcohol was made. So he knows his equipment and his craft.

***

The second day of our visit to Cooley, Becky had to stay at the B&B, suddenly running a high fever, of which I will tell more in a minute. Noel Sweeney is one of the nicest and funniest people I have met in the whiskey world thus far. He's been working in the industry since 1978 and acted as QA manager when the plant was closed in 1986. At the time he also had acquired experience with distilling vodka from neutral spirits. During our conversation, which took more

than four hours, he not only explained the different brands to me, but laced his stories with interesting anecdotes. Hence I learned that Billy Walker of BenRiach, GlenDronach and GlenGlassaugh fame, once worked as a consultant for Cooley.

I learned a lot more that memorable morning. With Teeling at the helm millions of Euros were poured into the dilapidated site while Irish Distillers (ID) was lurking in the distance, wondering what the new competitor was doing. In 1993 they knocked on the door and announced they were interested. This was an attractive proposition for Teeling, who urgently needed a new investment round in order to finance further growth. The board of directors approved ID's (read: Pernod Ricard's) bid, but then other powers were stirred. First the employees protested. They expected ID to immediately close down the distillery after the takeover. This fear was not without reason, since ID owned market leader Jameson and at the time produced number two – Tullamore Dew – for a third party. Then the Competition Authority reared its powerful head and managed to cancel the acquisition, reasoning that ID was already a virtual monopolist. In acquiring Cooley they would control 100% of the Irish whiskey production. Forget about Bushmills, then owned by Diageo, in this context, since that distillery is located in Northern Ireland.

The party was over, but not Cooley's financial problems. Fortunately at two minutes to twelve, two white knights came to the rescue. One of them was Heaven Hill, one of the major players in the American whiskey industry. This company bought vast amounts of maturing whiskey in advance. Cooley could grow on that financial injection.

Noel explains that many brands were launched, official distillery bottlings next to private label brands for third parties. Inishowen was re-introduced, next to Locke's, Miller's, Collins, Dun Leire, Writers' Tears (on of my personal favourites), The Wild Geese and a whole plethora of other fancy brand names, some new, some steeped in history. For the Japanese market Cooley even produced a whiskey called Hennessy. Thanks to Noel I now own a miniature. After four years the French Hennessy brand owner protested because the whiskey confused the consumer. After all, Hennessy is foremost known as a cognac. And whiskey is whiskey, even if it is matured in an ex-cognac cask.

Cooley has been making whiskey for various supermarket chains, among which Sainsbury, Tesco, Waitrose and Asda. They all carry whiskey under their own house label. Noel is responsible for all recipes and has room for much experimentation. When I ask, he smiles and answers: 'Deliver your own flavour profile and we make a whiskey to match that.' I nod, and make a note. Maybe that will serve well for a future expression in my series of annual single cask bottlings for my Dutch hometown Zwolle. Noel is a smooth and pleasant talker, who can go on and on, but I slightly begin to worry about Becky and propose a short break, which gives me the opportunity to check on her.

We stay in Ghan House, 10 minutes from the distillery by car. It's a picturesque medieval little town with a castle that once hosted King John, way back when in 1210. What remains of it is a ruins, towering over the town on a solitary rock. Ghan House itself is a perfect example of the Georgian architectural style and a little gem, built in 1727, surrounded by a wall with a sentinel tower attached to it.

On the first floor (or second, when you are an American) the restaurant has a marvellous rococo ceiling. It is open to non-residents. The first night I enjoyed a lobster bisque, halibut and a selection of Irish cheeses, accompanied by a bottle of Gewürztraminer. Alone. Becky was upstairs, drinking hot Irish made by our landlady, battling a fever.

Upon my return from the distillery, landlady Sarah opens

the door and informs me that she went for cough syrup and paracetamol at the pharmacy in Carlington. I go upstairs and find Becky, sleeping the sleep of the innocent and drive back to Cooley with a clean conscience.

Noel shows me the latest product of Cooley's. It is a new make of pure pot still whiskey, made at .... Locke's in Kilbeggan. Noel explains: things had gone well and Teeling could afford to purchase John Locke's distillery in Kilbeggan. At the time it was nothing more than a museum, beautifully restored by local people. Cooley took it back into production and currently it is the oldest working distillery in the world.

Locke's has a very interesting history of its own (see the last chapter of this book). With that story in mind, we said goodbye, after Noel had filled up a box with samples for Becky to try later.

***

In 2012 Cooley and Locke's were purchased by Beam Global, who had noticed a whopping 24% growth in sales of Irish whiskey in the USA. It also meant an end to my plans for a single cask bottling by Noel and me. Beam terminated the single cask program immediately, needing all available stocks for the USA.

Beam itself would be acquired in 2014 by the Japanese drinks giant Suntory, who had owned the Scottish single malt distilleries Auchentoshan, Bowmore and Glen Garioch for many years and could add Laphroaig to it, since that iconic single malt was part of Beam's portfolio too. So in the end, Cooley has become a world affair, with Scottish, Japanese and American siblings, bourbon and rye, at its side.

And Teeling? His sons Jack and Stephen are built of the same cloth, now proudly owning a newly built distillery in Dublin, baptised ... Teeling Distillery this time.

***

After two wonderful days we have to leave Ghan House. Becky dressed in layers of clothes, still not feeling well, but recovering. I seat her in the car very carefully and go inside to settle the bill. When I check it I remark that the medicines Sarah purchased for Becky are omitted. The sympathetic landlady waves her hand, answering: 'Included in the price of your stay, no worries', and she refuses to accept money for it. It's another example of that remarkable hospitality in Ireland, a phenomenon we encounter time and again during our entire Irish trip. I shake hands with Sarah and her husband Paul cordially, get in the car and head south, to our next historical treat.

Tout l'Amour with Irish Coffee

In 1829 the town of Tullamore, in the midlands of the Irish Republic, witnessed the foundation of an eponymous distillery built by Michael Molloy. When he died in 1857 his cousin Bernard Daly inherited the company, changing the name to B. Daly Distillery. Five years later, in 1862 a 14-year-old boy left his parents' farm to work at the distillery. He was partly paid in money, partly in kind, having been given a 'bedroom' on the hayloft above the stables. His name was Daniel Edmond Williams and his arrival would have far fetching consequences for the development of Tullamore, the town and its whiskey alike.

In the course of 25 years Williams managed to work his way up to the position of general manager at the distillery. Partly this was due to his work ethos, partly to Bernard's son, Captain Bernard Daly, Jr, who inherited the company when his father passed away. The Captain wasn't really interested in managing a distillery. Instead he preferred to play polo or a visit the horse races. In Williams he recognised an industrious person who soon implemented a series of important improvements.

In 1889 Tullamore could already reap the benefits of electricity and telephone. Williams branched out as well. He built a series of new warehouses, a bottling plant and a chain of 26 stores; he imported tea, exploited a wholesale store in grains and seeds. Eventually he even lent his name to the most important product of all, Tullamore Irish Whiskey, simply by adding his initials D.E.W. to it. From then on the whiskey from the town of Tullamore was advertised with 'Give every man his Dew'.

Until a few years ago, when I decided to make a serious study of Irish whiskey and its history, I thought the extension of the brand name referred to the dew on the fields surrounding Tullamore. Don't blame me, I do like this dram and for me it resembles that fine mist of dewdrops one can find on green meadows early in the morning.

In 1903 D.E. Williams became the major shareholder and Tullamore kept growing as a brand name and in market share. But the tide would turn, due to that series of historical events that would bring the Irish whiskey industry to the brink of perdition: World War I (1914-1918), Prohibition in the USA (1920-1933), the economic wars with England (1930s) and World War II (1938-1945).

As one of very few, Tullamore Dew withstood this string of disasters, sometimes balancing on the abyss, but never falling. D.E.W.'s grandson Desmond had taken over the helm and decided to venture in the field of product innovation. In 1974 Irish Mist was launched, a whiskey liqueur based on an old recipe belonging to a clan chief from the 17th century, as the story goes. With Europe recovering and rebuilding after the war, it seemed applicable to restore a 250-year-old drink containing whiskey, herbs and honey.

Desmond was among the first to realise the importance of blended whiskeys next to the production of the indigenous, more distinctive pure pot still whiskeys. He would also profit from an invention from Joe Sheridon, head chef at Foynes airbase, the precursor to Shannon Airport. The story goes that a group of exhausted American passengers arrived on a Pan Am flying boat on a miserable winter evening, thinking they were there for refuelling but forced to stay the night. They needed a fortifying drink to warm them and calm their nerves. Sheridan decided to add a splash of whiskey to their coffee, put in two spoons of brown sugar and topped it with thick cream. When tasting it, his customers asked if it was Brazilian coffee. He answered with the now legendary words: 'This is *Irish* coffee!' Mainly due to Stanton

Delaplane, a travel writer for the *San Francisco Chronicle*, the drink became very popular in no time. Just a few years after the seemingly insignificant event at Shannon airport, Irish coffee was served in the bars of San Francisco. The whiskey Sheridan had used and proscribed was reportedly ... Tullamore Dew.

In the end these successes would not save the distillery. In 1959 the gates were closed and the brand was sold to Powers. Production was outsourced to a distillery near Cork. The following decade saw a series of mergers and fusions, culminating in the foundation of the Irish Distillers Group in 1972. Until very recently Tullamore Dew was still being made near Cork, at Pernod's Midleton plant, home of competitor Jameson's. And the French pronounce the brand name such as something sounding like Tout l'Amour. However in 1994 the brand name was sold to C&C International, who kept outsourcing production in Midleton. In 2010 WM Grants & Sons, founders of Glenfiddich and Balvenie, acquired Tullamore Dew, but still had it made in Midleton. Until September 2014 when the Grants built a brand new distillery in the town of Tullamore. The water shortage plaguing the site was solved by laying a 14 kilometre pipe from the Slieve Bloom Mountains. The new 'pot still' wash still [for spirit from a mix of malted and unmalted barley] was modelled after the original Tullamore version, on display at Kilbeggan Distillery. The entire complex is modern, beautiful, efficient and built with expansion in mind, as I could see for myself when visiting the place in the Spring of 2016.

***

During our 2010 journey we could enjoy a visit to the Tullamore Dew Heritage centre, which would be carefully restored by the new owners. At the end of that visit we were

195

presented with an Irish coffee and left for Killenard to check into a five-star golf and spa resort of the same name. At the time they were building up a whiskey collection in order to apply for membership in the Irish Whiskey Trail. Dinner was scheduled for the Fisherman's Thatched Pub, a place hard to find, so a taxi is more than welcome. Upon arrival publican Sean Ward, opens the door and welcomes us with the words: 'This place is in the middle of nowhere ... and at the centre of everything.' This is not only the local pub but also a real village community gathering place where colourful people come and go, locals and strangers alike. At the bar we are entertained by a female travel writer who lives around the corner, but just returned from a trip in the Far East. Later in the evening we have an encounter with a ghost, who captures the attention of all guests. It turns out to be a harmless one, but it was a bit creepy. We're happy when the taxi arrives to bring us back to the Killenard.

The next morning we continue our pub crawl with a visit to Mooney's in Monasterevan. Owner Paul Hyland is quite an entrepreneur. The pub is divided into three different sections. The front part is a tiny convenience store, the middle part the actual pub and the back part a funeral parlour. With a possible motto 'Eat, Drink & Die', Paul seems to have created a one-stop-shop. He explains that Irish pubs have long been used to host the wakes of the deceased in a village or small town. About two decades ago the owner of the funeral parlour decided to quit – his business that is – and Paul took over. He asks if I am interested in a coffin myself and opens a shed behind the pub. 'These are my standard models', he proudly points at eight different types. Take your pick!' We politely but decidedly decline his kind offer and walk back into the pub, where Paul shows us the one surviving bottle of Cassidy whiskey in the world. A unique piece that we enthusiastically photograph.

The buildings of Cassidy distillery, or what's left thereof, can be found in the village and Paul directs us where to go. We digitally immortalise the mighty warehouses that are sadly ruined beyond restoration. A few years ago an attempt was made to turn the ground floors into a series of little boutique shops. An attempt that failed miserably. Rather melancholy, we return to our car and cover a 60 kilometre stretch before our next stop.

LOCKE'S
Old Kilbeggan
WHISKEY
PURE OLD POT STILL

Distilled Bottled & Guaranteed

by

JOHN LOCKE & CO., LTD.,
BRUSNA DISTILLERY

KILBEGGAN
Estd. 1757

70° PROOF

Locke's Kilbeggan – A Time Warp?

Kilbeggan is a little town in the heart of the Irish Republic. It is situated roughly 55 miles west of Dublin, along the main road to Galway. This is a place where whiskey has been crafted for ages.

Brusna Distillery was erected in 1757, named after Brusna House and the little river passing the distillery, whose current was used to generate energy via the large water wheel attached to the outer wall of the building. The founder was a man named Matthew McManus. He ran the distillery for almost 40 years, after which period he sold the company to George Codd and concentrated on producing beer instead. His main reason was the fact that much more tax was imposed upon whiskey distilling than beer brewing. McManus had also lost his direct descendants and heirs. Two sons died in 1798, as members of the Rebel Army of the Free Irish. Another son, who had been sent to France by his father to receive a formal education, came back with a mind full of rebellious ideas and was later hanged for high treason.

The Codd family expanded the business. Part of the expansion can still be seen in the present entrance to the distillery. John Locke took over the company in 1846, giving it his own name. Until 1921 three consecutive John Locke's held the reigns of the business. That wasn't always a smooth ride. John II died at a relatively young age, leaving his widow Mary Anne at the helm. Se was assisted by her own family who possessed a nearby brewery, until her sons John Edward and James Harvey came of age. The two brothers were responsible for the considerable growth of Locke's in the second part of the 19th century.

From the beginning, energy had been generated by the giant water wheel. There was a downside to it, since the river

regularly ran dry in summer. So, in 1887 it was decided to add a steam boiler as a backup. The distillery prospered and Mary Anne set her fortune to local causes. She founded the Convent of Mercy in 1879 and was instrumental in the building of Kilbeggan Racecourse. To this day it is still a popular horse racetrack. In 1883 approximately 120 people had found a job at Locke's, which made the company the largest employer in the region.

The Locke's were a pious lot and even had a private chapel built in Brusna House. However, this didn't restrict the brothers to living according to Catholic dogma. James Harvey was a confirmed bachelor throughout his life and kept a mistress on the side for many years –Florence Savage (what's in a name?). Her sister Mary would marry John Edward in 1880. They had two daughters – again a Florence and a Mary – but the marriage was not a great success. Mother Mary was rather promiscuous and entertained various gentlemen in the area, which led poor John Edward to kick her off the premises a mere five years later. They were officially divorced before the Probate and Matrimonial Court in Dublin in 1896. The Locke's were part of the landed gentry so this story was the talk of the town in the deeply Catholic Ireland of the time. To avoid further gossip and speculations the family quickly came to an agreement favouring the future of both children. Mother Mary moved to a country house in the vicinity of Kilbeggan with her daughters Florence and Mary, also known as Sweets. The promiscuous mother had a nickname too: Muds. She loved to ride horses and encouraged her daughters to do the same. Later Muds would become known as the first woman owning and driving a motorcar in County Westmeath. She was rather a character and wanted to be recognised for who she thought she was. Once she drove her car over the big toe of a police officer and told him loudly and clearly that he shouldn't put it in her path the next time. When shopping in Dublin she had the habit of entering a store and clearly announcing, 'I am Mrs. Locke!' When the staff didn't react immediately she would become severely irritated. To be fair it has to be said that Muds had some good character traits. During the First World War she worked with heart and soul for the Red Cross in various hospitals in France, for which help she would later receive a medal from the French. Upon her return to Ireland she became Commander of the Westmeath Auxiliary Red Cross Hospital in nearby Mullingar.

Unfortunately in the early years of the 20th century the distillery was going downhill. The Locke's had invested heavily in exporting whiskey to the USA. When Prohibition went nationwide in 1920, they lost a huge market. Not long after that event John Edward died and James Harvey had to run the company on his own. When he passed away in 1927 all shares came into the hands of Muds, Sweets and Florence. The latter wasn't very much involved in the day-to-day business, but the other two were. Muds would reign until her death in 1940 and Sweets became the general manager at the mature age of 57. Throughout her life she had been more interested in horse riding and leisure, neglecting the financial and commercial side of the business. In 1947 the sisters decided to sell the distillery, unwittingly to a group of con artists. The deal fell through, however, when the deposit money failed to arrive. The following scandal, blown out of proportion by a politician, severely damaged the distillery's reputation and chances of sale. In 1953 the stills went silent for good due to a tax increase on spirits and in 1958 closure followed. The buildings were rented out to a German who used them as a Mercedes garage and a pigsty. Locke's Distillery seemed to have died definitively.

But no, in 1982 its fate changed. A small group of enthusiasts in Kilbeggan decided to restore the old distillery.

Under the engaging management of Brian and Bernadette Quinn the first steps were made. Brian had been employed by a company that had purchased the former distillery buildings in which to assemble machinery, so he knew what he was in for. The Quinns bought and moved into the old Locke mansion opposite the distillery. Inhabitants of Kilbeggan donated time, money and old artefacts, of which various ones are on display today in the attic of the malt barn. With love, patience, dedication and passion the entire complex was restored to its former glory. A group of volunteers spent more than two years rebuilding the steam engine, which now runs a few times a year for special events. The water wheel is turning and again generates the energy for the equipment inside, just as it must have done in the 18th century.

With the purchase of Cooley by Beam in 2012, the oldest working distillery in the world went into American ownership, but only for a few years. With the acquisition of Beam by Japan's drinks giant Suntory in 2014, Kilbeggan now is part of a conglomerate that owns other brands like Laphroaig, Bowmore, Makers Mark and Jim Beam. With the latter one we're back where we started with this book, in Kentucky. What better end than coming full circle?

However, there may be a *Still Stories II* in the future ...

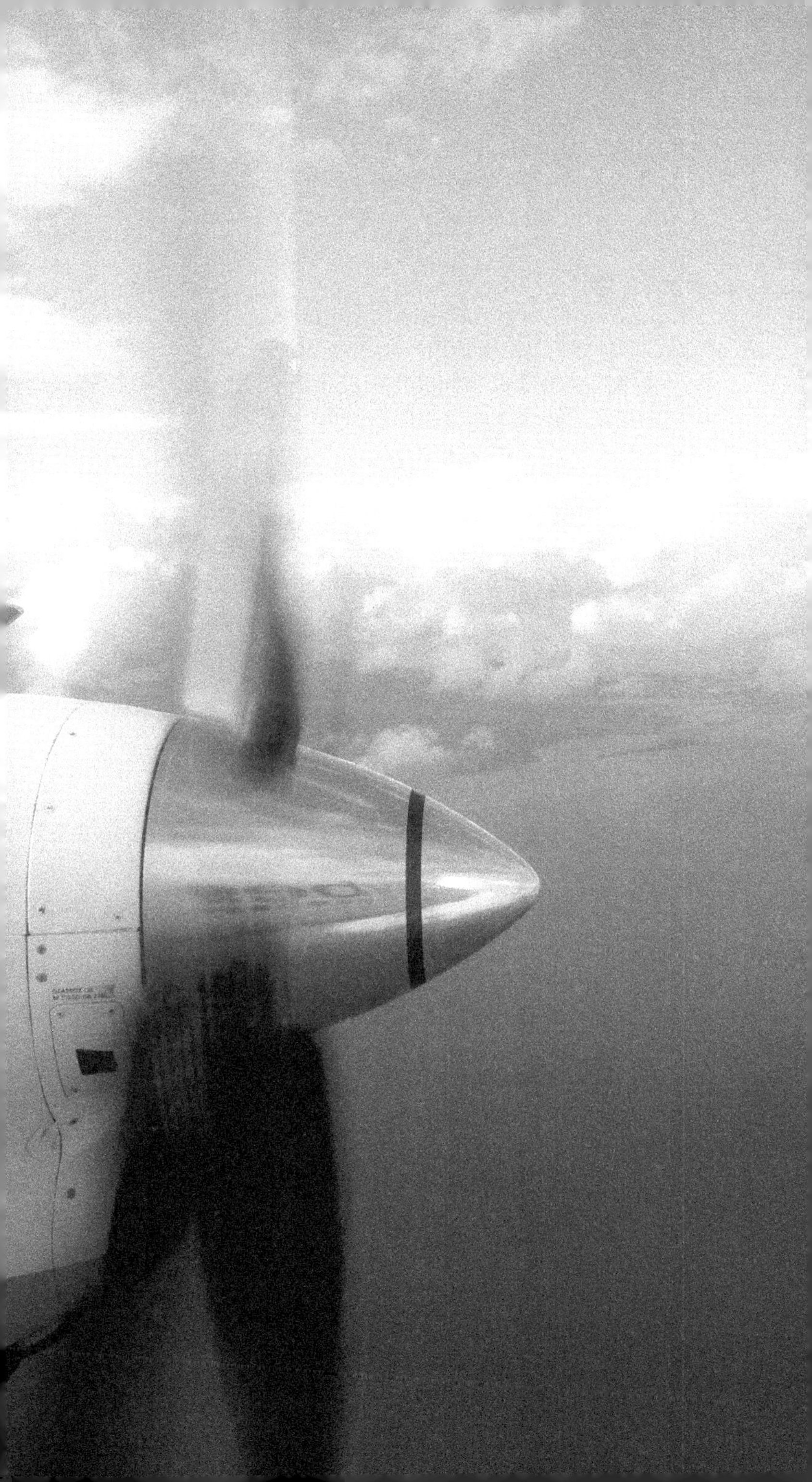

Photo Registry

Other English-language Books from the Author

1815-2015 - 200 Years of Laphroaig
Bourbon & Blues
The Craigellachie Collection of Whisky Labels
A Field Guide to Whisky *
The House
The Legend of Laphroaig
The Malt Log
Malts & Jazz
Raising the Kursk
The Road to Craigellachie
Rum & Reggae
A Taste of Whisky
Whisky & Jazz

Contributions
30-Second Whisky (Charles MacLean et al.) *
101 Whiskies to Try Before You Die (Ian Buxton)
1001 Whiskies (Dominic Roskrow et al.)
Beer Hunter, Whisky Chaser (Ian Buxton et al.)
Whisky – Eyewitness Guide (Charles MacLean et al.)
Whisky – The World Atlas (Dave Broom)
WORLD WHISKY (Charles MacLean et al.)

See also: www.hansoffringa.com

* Scheduled for publication in 2017